Living In the Freedom Frequency

Raise Your Vibration & Live Above the Line

Karen of the Klassen family

Living In The Freedom Frequency

Raise Your Vibration & Live Above the Line

Editing by Norma Jean Maxwell and Esther Sarlo

Formatting by Bojan Kratofil

Cover Design by GermanCreative

For inquiries, please contact: Karen of the Klassen family

www.karenklassen.ca

ISBN: 978-0-9918890-1-3

Third Edition

Acknowledgments

I am grateful to all the beautiful souls who have been there through my most challenging times and supported me on my journey of awakening to my true purpose and passion.

A special thank you to:

My family for being my greatest teachers on my path to unconditional love.

To all my soul sisters and brothers who are on this journey beyond the familiar. You are the Life Force of this earth and together we are standing strong in the fullest expression of our divine authority.

You are the ones who inspire me to do the great work I am here to do.

Together We Rise!

To all the earth angels who are here to co-create heaven on earth.

Table of Contents

Introduction

What relationship do you have with the thoughts or voices in your head? Those voices that tell you what to do, how to act, or how you should be? Did you know that you have two main voices? You have one voice that lies to you and says, *you are not good enough, you don't know enough,* or *you are not lovable.* The other voice only speaks truth and is here to remind you that you *are loved by the universe and that you are a unique, individualized expression of the Creator.*

Just like a garden, if your mind is not carefully tended, the weeds will take over and bury all the goodness that was seeded long ago.

Many of us have forgotten about the gardens of our minds and have unconsciously or consciously allowed a negative force to take over.

This introduction is a glimpse into my past and why I was drawn to write this book. Each chapter offers you powerful tools to prepare you to listen to a new voice within, the voice that has been whispering to you, seeking to set you free from the darkness, the struggle, and the hardship.

My Story

I grew up in an authoritarian household governed by the rule of, "Do as I Say, Not as I Do." Even as a youngster, I was frustrated with how my mother and father communicated by constantly yelling, pointing fingers, arguing about everything, and then avoiding each other for days. I desperately craved attention. I wanted to be acknowledged, to be seen and especially understood by my mother and father. I was called a crybaby every time I showed tears. I had no idea how to handle the conflicting energies between my mother and father and no matter what I said, I felt small and insecure.

I was a good kid, which meant keeping my room clean, never talking back, always doing what was asked of me, doing well in school, and never getting into trouble. My escape was spending all my spare time riding my horse.

Everything began to change as I grew into a rebellious teenager. My mother and father, especially my mother, began to transfer their unhappiness onto me. Having one of them yelling was challenging enough, but to have both of them joining forces in a barrage of cruel words directed at me was more than my soul could bear. At the time, I did not have the understanding that they were using me as a scapegoat to transfer all the emotional pain.

I believe there is a defining moment when the ego veils the light of the soul. I remember that moment vividly. I was sitting on the floor while my mother and father stood over me yelling and blaming me for their unhappiness. Up until that moment I had been a well-behaved kid, but now, everything changed.

In the midst of my deep sadness and tears I heard a voice, a voice that did not belong to my mom or dad. I listened again. To my surprise, it was coming from inside my body. The voice spoke again so clearly there was no way I could misinterpret its message. The voice said, "Do you want me to take care of you?"

My mother and father continued to yell at me from above and threatened to send me to a psychiatric hospital. Seriously, they wanted to send me away because I cried too much? The fear of being sent away, leaving the only family I knew, paralyzed my mind and my body. I had no idea how to cope with the situation. Did crying make me a bad girl? The voice within spoke again, "Let me take care of you. I will make you strong."

I could not stop crying, and in the midst of the hurt and a longing to feel loved and accepted, I answered the voice with a "Yes." With permission granted, I instantly felt a rush of energy move through my body. I could not believe the power I was feeling. My tears instantly dried up. I felt as if something had just taken over my body. I felt strong. This inner strength was incredible. I felt all fear vanish. I looked up at my mother and father and I was no longer afraid of them. They now just looked like two puppets on strings. I could see their mouths moving but I could not hear their words. I slid my back up the wall. Now standing, I felt powerful. Invincible! A smile came over my face. I no longer cared what my mother and father thought or said to me, as my love for them vanished into thin air. I no longer cared about anything. I felt so good. I felt free. I just looked at them both, smiled, told them I was leaving and walked out. A darkness had taken over my soul.

I did come back that evening, physically; however, they never saw that innocent little girl again. I enjoyed my newfound power for many years as my dark self possessed my life. It showed me the path of drugs, alcohol, and sex that would feed my inner demons. I was shown the power to manipulate, to hate, to resent, and to deceive. I discovered the power in pretending I was someone else. I could become the shy girl, the innocent girl, or the mean girl. I was like a chameleon, and I knew how to get my way. The light of my soul was buried for many years as the destructive force of darkness within created many walls around my heart, concealing the truth of who I am.

My inner demons (what I now refer to as my inner *Fallen Angels*) began to grow in strength and create havoc in my life. I was kind to others only if I knew they had something I wanted. All I wanted to do was get high.

When I was nineteen, I moved to the city where I found others just like me. I was on welfare. I hated life. I know hate is a strong word but that was my state of mind at the time. I blamed everyone else for my loneliness, for my suffering, and for the dull and mundane life I was living. I had already been raped twice but because I was so unaware, I did not even identify it as rape until much later in life. I hated my body. I was addicted to drugs and alcohol, and I only associated with others who were as lost and alone as I was. In my twenties, I married an abusive drug dealer and was now in a job that was deeply unfulfilling. I suffered from chronic back pain, scoliosis, Irritable Bowel Syndrome, allergies, fatigue, depression, and continuous suicidal thoughts. Doctors told me that if I didn't change my life, I would be dead by the time I was thirty.

Thankfully, I had a spiritual revelation in 1993—a direct experience of God (Source). I was at home, sick with a cold, and feeling sorry for myself. I had just watched Shirley MacLaine's movie, *Out on a Limb,* and was contemplating my life. Questions I had never asked myself before began to surface: "Who am I?" and "Why am I here?" Within moments, I sensed the energy in my living room change. I felt a profound sensation wash over my body and it intensified with every second, as if a lightning bolt was surging through every cell, vibrating every atom of my being. Fear rose up briefly, only to be replaced with a blanket of the most beautiful love enveloping me, a love beyond anything I had ever known. I became aware of the part of me that was whole and had never experienced pain, harm, or suffering. I felt connected to all of life and knew my soul came to this beautiful planet for a higher purpose. Then, as fast as this experience occurred, it disappeared.

As I looked around my living room, I felt dazed, confused, and wondered what had just happened? I still felt the highly charged energy on my skin as all the hair on my arms stood straight up. I felt different. I wanted to feel this profound love again. Then I heard a voice from within, like a thought with the volume turned up. With full clarity it said, "Relinquish all fear that limits you."

From that moment onward, my life shifted dramatically. Where once I could only see darkness, suffering, loss, and despair, I now saw the truth: that all beings have been given the divine power to create heaven on earth for themselves. In order to experience heaven on earth for myself, it was essential that I create heaven in my mind first.

I now had a hunger to learn, to know more. I began a journey beyond the familiar. I was on a quest of self-discovery and I had this persistent desire to feel and connect with this higher love again, a love I now refer to as *Enlightened Love*. I knew this higher love would set me free of all the mental, emotional, and physical pain I had created for myself.

My purpose in writing this book is to share with you the journey I took in transforming my life from the emotional, mental, and physical pain that nearly destroyed me, to living in the higher worlds of love and freedom. I will show you that by making small shifts in how you view yourself and the world around you, you can transform your life in profound ways. I will show you the possibilities available to you, and all you are asked to do is apply and integrate these higher thoughts into your life.

I am not a doctor, a psychiatrist, or psychologist. I can only share my experiences with you and what has empowered me in becoming the woman I am today. Through many years of self-discipline and devotion to my spiritual calling, I was able to transform my once diseased body into a healthy body, free from pain and drugs. I am now also free of the negative emotions and the dark voices that once consumed me. I have transformed my relationships with my mother, father and brother, and I have created a successful business doing what I love.

In this book, I will introduce you to a whole new way of seeing, feeling and experiencing your emotions. I will also show you how you can free yourself from negative emotions and qualities that may be sabotaging your relationships or holding you back from experiencing the love and joy that is rightfully yours. In these pages, I offer 80 Higher Thoughts. Each one can be used as a life guide or reference tool to empower you in every area of your life. You are here to live above the line and connect to a higher intelligence that holds the blueprint to living in the Freedom Frequency of life.

Note: As you read through these chapters, I will refer to *Selves* (with an uppercase S) as aspects of you that resonate above the line, in the Frequency of Freedom, and *selves* (with a lowercase s) as aspects of you that resonate below the line, in the Frequency of Fear.

For each *Higher Idea*, I invite you to contemplate the words expressed and think of them as inspired action steps you can take right now. I recommend that you read the entire book first, as each chapter prepares you for the next. Then, once completed, feel free to open the book any day of the week. Whatever page you open, you will see your unique *Higher Idea* for that day.

If you commit to bringing each of these 80 Higher Ideas into your life, you will notice an incredible transformation as you spiral up and live above the line in the Freedom Frequency of life.

I love and appreciate my mother and father, and I am grateful to my soul for saying "yes" to being birthed in such an environment so I could learn the life lessons required for my own awakening.

In the Spirit of Oneness,

Karen of the Klassen family

Chapter One
Journey Beyond the Familiar

Are you ready to remember the truth of who you are? Are you ready to experience more fulfilling relationships in which you are accepted for who you are? Are you ready to reclaim your power and stand for what you believe in?

If you said, "Yes" to any of the above questions, then congratulations! You are ready to dive deep into the most fascinating journey you will ever take, *a journey beyond the familiar.*

We are in the midst of a shift in consciousness where we are moving from a fear-based world of stress, uncertainty, and anger to living above the line in the frequency of freedom, love, peace of mind, and abundance for all.

We all experience loss, pain, and suffering at some point in our lives. If we are open to learning our life lessons, even in the most difficult of times, it is possible to see that all experience is an opportunity for us to open our hearts to love, acceptance, and embracing a deeper truth. This book is for those of you — if you are ready to spiral up into living a heart-centered life.

I believe you are not flawed, you do not have faults, and you are not *"just a human being."* You are Divinely perfect just as you are. I believe we are all Divinely perfect. However, not perfect in the egoic definition of the word. Perfection from an ego perspective is when we *pretend* we are happy and we do not tell the truth about how we feel or the problems we are facing. This is the opposite of Divine perfection.

Divine perfection means letting go of judgments about yourself. It means being truthful with yourself right here, right now in the moment, and seeing that the YOU that is here, whether you are sad, afraid, happy, unfulfilled, laughing, angry, or content, *is* Divinely perfect. Being true to yourself will spiral you up to higher levels of consciousness.

I trust that God has not made any mistakes – therefore I believe you are Divinely Perfect. Since you were created in the image of the Creator, then you are, by definition, *Divinely perfect.* Every thought, word, or experience you have had or are having *is* in divine order for the emergence and evolution of your soul—and for all Divine beings.

You may have been taught to see yourself as average, imperfect, or weak because you may not be experiencing the full manifestation of your dreams yet. What would become possible if you stop striving for perfection and instead begin to see that your soul is already

Divinely perfect? Begin to see that you are loved by the Universe, no matter what. You are a gift to the world. You are *living art*. Everything is divinely orchestrated for you to recognize to the essence of who you really are—*a divine being.*

The reason there is so much misery, struggle, and tragedy in our lives is because we have forgotten this truth. We have separated ourselves from our own divine nature. We fear the unknown because we don't know what it looks like, or we think we may not be loved and appreciated for who we really are. Why have we made our own happiness, freedom, and GREATNESS something to be so afraid of?

Another reason we hold ourselves back is the belief that if we choose *growth* and *spiritual fulfillment,* we will leave our loved ones behind. How about a higher idea that no one is *ever* left behind? I believe every soul is travelling on a unique journey beyond the familiar and is evolving at its own pace.

Every being is on his or her spiritual path, whether consciously aware of it or not. We are all moving through a spiritual metamorphosis, from living a fear-based life of negative thinking to a love-centered life of pure positive Source energy. I believe this way of life is possible for all, and many on this earth plane are already experiencing a heart-centered life and showing the way.

The analogy of the caterpillar becoming a butterfly is often used to help us understand our own progression through the life-transformation process. In order to complete their metamorphoses into butterflies, caterpillars create a chrysalis where their cells begin to resonate at a higher frequency. Their current form breaks down, leaving them vulnerable. This vulnerability phase creates the space for something new to be birthed—*a butterfly*. Just as the evolutionary blueprint to transform exists within the caterpillar, the blueprint to transform from one identity to another exists within YOU.

You may be going through your own metamorphosis now, and it may feel agonizing as you move through the uncomfortable energy of vulnerability. Remember, the caterpillar does not make itself into a butterfly. It seeks the butterfly within. As you seek to unveil your *Higher Self,* your new cells begin to dissolve the 'current you' to reveal your wings of freedom—you become *an earth angel!*

Moving from where you are (your current reality) to where you want to be (your preferred reality) involves a desire for mental, emotional, and spiritual growth along with a willingness to dive in and remember who you are. Since you are here reading this book, you obviously have a hunger to expand your awareness and embrace a heart-centered life. I invite you to stay open as we immerse ourselves deeper with every page. Breathe in what resonates with you—and what does not, just exhale.

There are many paths you can take that will lead you through the unknown and into your preferred reality (or a higher plane of consciousness.) I am here to promote self-leadership, so I urge you to follow your own path and connect to your inner Divine guides and teachers. I am only here to remind you of what you may have forgotten – a power lies inside you that can enhance your relationships, create optimal health, and bring more abundance and harmony into your life. This book is a reference tool to empower you to journey through uncharted regions of your mind and to connect to the Divine intelligence that exists in your heart.

Keep reading and stay curious.

Higher Idea #1 Give Yourself the Gift of Time

Before we go too deep, let's talk about one thing first—*Time*. How often do you say to your friends or family, *"I don't have time"* or *"I am too busy?"*

A great life also requires *time* to be created; however, we can get caught up in the idea of *I am too busy* or *I don't have time to learn something new.*

Do you believe time is speeding up or slowing down?

What if you discovered that you have the power to expand or contract time? Yes, your mind is very powerful, and it is your thoughts and feelings that create your experiences.

Now, you may be juggling the many responsibilities of being a mother or father or being in a relationship or being a business owner with a very large "To-Do" list. I get it!

Our everyday stresses and responsibilities can keep us trapped in the *busyness* of life. I know there are only twenty-four hours in a day and maybe your "To-Do" list is a mile long. But what if the next time you catch yourself saying, *"I am too busy"* or *"I don't have time,"* you stop everything you are doing? Just stop! Take a moment to breathe, and then ask yourself the question, *"If I am the creator of my routine, when did I allow my routine to take over my life?"*

Now breathe into the word *busy* and the phrase *I don't have time.* Expand your awareness to notice how these words make you feel. Do you feel constriction, or do you feel expansion? The word *busy* carries the vibration of chaos and stress. With all this *busyness,* how can you have time to nurture your mind, body, and spirit? The answer is: Only *you* can create time for yourself. If you are caught up in the vibration of *busyness,* you may have forgotten that you are the one who created your busy schedule in the first place. Your *busyness* is a learned behavior and now you can unlearn what is not working for you.

For some reason, you have allowed your Busy self to take over your life and this self can cause you to believe that if you are not busy doing, doing, doing, everything will fall apart. Is this true? A heart-centered life is a balance of *doing (masculine energy)* and *being (feminine energy).*

You have the power to create your day exactly as you want it to be. I suggest you view time from a higher perspective. See and know that time is fluid, not linear. Time constricts when your thinking is constricted. Time expands when you feel expansion of your spirit. At the core of who you are is an ageless, eternal being unbound by time.

Many years ago, I stopped wearing a watch. Why? Because as long as I was time-bound, I found it more challenging to live in the present moment. The more I made the choice to live in the moment, the more I experienced time expanding. I now live on Divine time (listening to my inner clock), and I know that I am always successfully engaged in the right activity, and there is plenty of time for everything. There is only *now.*

Today's Higher Idea: Release your Busy self (below the line) and welcome your Creative Self (above the line). You are now releasing chaos from your life. Substitute the word "busy" with words that resonate at a higher frequency such as *creative, active,* or *full.* You can say, *"I have a full day ahead of me"* or *"I have plenty of time for everything."*

Higher Idea #2 Define What Freedom Is to You

Now that you have plenty of time to read and explore the Freedom Frequency of life, let's explore the word *freedom*. What does *freedom* mean to you? Freedom means different things to men and women. Some want to be financially free, while others want to be free from materialism. This book embraces the ideas that true freedom is the opportunity to be fully who you are and create the life that lives in your heart. This includes the freedom of all mental, emotional, and physical pain.

Many of us do not know how to handle the vast power of freedom; for this reason, we have so many laws and rules. Fear creates distrust and separation. This can cause us to react to life and then cause harm to others, to steal from others, or take advantage of those less fortunate. We abuse freedom by trying to control others, which we do when we experience a deep feeling of emptiness within and a disconnection from life.

You gain freedom the more you live in the present moment and when you deepen into truth and allow yourself to see the bigger picture of life. You gain freedom when you stop arguing with life and surrender to *what is*, to what life *is* in the moment and not judge it as wrong, right, good, or bad. Trust that what you are experiencing is a part of your soul's contract—*what you agreed to come into this life to express.* Everything is happening for a higher purpose. Life is about expansion and growth. Having acceptance for where you are allows for judgment to dissolve.

You are not alone. It may feel at times that your soul is chained in a dungeon and that darkness is all you see. You are not the darkness. Freedom from pain and suffering, from lack and limitation is here for you. There is a way out of the pit of life. Freedom is your inherent birthright.

Today's Higher Idea: A simple visualization that will raise your vibration instantly is to visualize yourself climbing a ladder up out of the darkness, then place your feet on solid ground and stand in the sun—the light of integration. Do you feel a shift in how you feel? Your mind is where your power lives and knowing how to use your higher mind, your Divine Mind, will bring you the freedom you seek.

Higher Idea #3 The Law of Vibration

The Law of Attraction is based on the scientific theory that says everything in the universe is based on energy. The Law of Attraction states that whatever you choose to think about, negative or positive, is what you will attract into your life. You attract into your life what you focus on.

The results you are experiencing in your relationships, business, health, finances, etc., are a direct result of the Law of Attraction at work, whether or not you are conscious of it. The Law of Attraction is always present in every choice you make. If you are not manifesting what you want, it is because your thoughts are focusing on *what is not working* instead of what you want your life to be. For example, if you want your relationship to improve, it is wise to focus on what you want your relationship to *look* and *feel* like instead of focusing on what your beloved is doing wrong. Whatever you focus on, *you get more of.*

In order to fully understand the Law of Attraction, you need to understand another universal law: the Law of Vibration. The Law of Vibration is the foundation of the Law of Attraction. The Law of Vibration, simply put, is that everything in our universe is made up of energy—energy vibrations that transmit a frequency.

In his book, *Ageless Body, Timeless Mind,* Deepak Chopra reminds us that our bodies appear to be composed of solid matter that can be broken down into molecules and atoms. Quantum physics tells us that every atom is more than 99.9999 percent empty space, and the subatomic particles moving at lightning speed through this space are actually bundles of vibrating energy.

Everything, including *your physical body,* is vibrating at a specific frequency. Every atom in your cells sends out an electromagnetic wave, a *vibration,* and it is this vibration of your thoughts and feelings that is transmitted into your external world, which then creates your physical experience. For example, when you are drawn to be in a relationship, you will attract someone who has the same vibrational match as your unresolved subconscious issues. This is why being in a relationship offers you the perfect opportunity for spiritual and emotional growth. You attract a mirror of you to help you clear out lower energy vibrations so you can spiral up and spread your wings.

Energy is always in a state of motion, and we have the ability to control that motion through our *emotions,* which we will explore in Chapter Two. If you want the Law of Attraction to work in your favour, then become aware of your own *emotional vibration.*

When you live above the line, your emotional vibration is high, and you attract what your heart desires. To live above the line, requires a shift in your beliefs. If you don't believe you have the power to manifest more love, joy, or peace in your life, then you will not have the positive emotions required to attract it. If your thoughts are vibrating in alignment with your heart's desires, then it will be easier for you to feel excited about manifesting more of what you want. If your thoughts vibrate below the line, your manifestation abilities may be lacking. When you are vibrating above the line, you manifest with ease and grace. This is where your magic lives.

Today's Higher Idea: Share with someone your understanding of the Law of Vibration and how it applies to your life.

Higher Idea #4 Live Above the Line

You may be wondering what it means to *Live Above the Line.* Since every thought, feeling, word, action, or behaviour vibrates at a certain frequency, that can either spiral you down toward death or up toward more life, it would be a higher idea to know and embody those that spiral you up above the line. To simplify, I created *The Freedom Frequency Chart* on the next page to show the many vibrations within each of the two core frequencies that represent the foundation of this book: The Frequency of Fear and The Frequency of Freedom.

You will see that below the horizontal line is a small list of perceived negative emotions, actions, or behaviours we experience as women and men. These lower energies can make you feel very uncomfortable and can cause you to take actions you would not otherwise take, because at the core of all negative emotions is FEAR. For example, fear of being judged, fear of being rejected, fear of losing control, fear of not being good enough, fear of being misunderstood, and so on.

Above the line is where you experience the higher expressions of life such as joy, abundance, and love that you, I am sure, want to experience more of. *You are meant to LIVE ABOVE THE LINE!* Unfortunately, many of us only experience brief moments of these higher energies because we have not been taught how to spiral up and fully receive these higher vibrations of life.

Both the Frequency of Freedom and the Frequency of Fear consist of electromagnetic fields of energy vibrations. You tune into this information the same way you tune into your favourite radio station. Each frequency relates to states of mind or levels of consciousness.

Living above the line is about making a conscious choice to spiral up from living in the lower realms of negative emotions and darker forces (fear) that can destroy your relationships, your business pursuits, and your life.

The Freedom Frequency Chart

Positive Emotions and Qualities that resonate in the Freedom Frequency are:

trust	commitment	oneness	care
compassion	bliss	appreciation	empowerment
integrity	ecstasy	health	luxury
honour	connected	divine order	ease and grace
joy	synchronicity	passion	authentic
happiness	genuine	courage	passionate
respect	wealth	knowing	romantic
admired	abundance	truth	relaxed
loyalty	wholeness	remember	playful
peace	gratitude	calm	simplicity
thoughtful	valued	strength	celebration
growth	worthy	observer	
laughter	willingness	certainty	
	union	patience	

Negative Emotions and Qualities that resonate in the Fear Frequency are:

stress	unworthy	anger	hate
frustration	despair	jealousy	sympathy
worry	abandonment	hope	pity
unappreaciated	fatigue	pain	chaos
exhaustion	empty	limitation	rage
neglect	hurt	lack	shame
self doubt	humiliation	manipulation	helplessness
loneliness	confused	deception	greed
depression	discouraged	needy	resistance
anxiety	sabotage	desperate love	struggle
raclsm	uncertainty	guilt	disappointment
suffering	resentment	ashamed	disease

Figure 1

We have been living in a world of polarity, a world of opposites: negative and positive, good and evil, dark and light, or fear and love.

As we evolve, we transition out of this world of polarity, third dimensional living, into higher dimensional experiences. The illusion of separation begins to dissolve, and we once again come into alignment with the truth — that we are all *one*.

You are being called to step into a grander vision of who you are, to become conscious of the multi-dimensional aspects of intelligence within, and then align with the highest version of who you are—your *Divine nature.*

Living above the line will change how you view your emotions, how you view your relationships, and how you view yourself and your life. Your perceptions of reality will shift in very profound ways as you become aware of a reality that is much bigger than you've ever imagined.

Unfortunately, many of us find the journey to freedom too uncomfortable so we make the choice to stay locked up in the predictable patterns of avoidance and live by default. I know because I lived by default for most of the early part of my life. I was unaware of my power within or how my negative thoughts and feelings created all the pain, low self-esteem, and lack of love and freedom in my life. I was completely unaware of how I had allowed fear to control my life. Having a direct experience of *enlightened love* woke me up to the truth of reality, and making the commitment to *live my spirituality* has been one of the biggest gifts I have ever given myself.

Today's Higher Idea: Develop a daily practice of expanding your awareness of when you are vibrating below the line and how different your life would be if you lived above the line. Observe yourself without judgment.

Higher Idea #5 Vibrate in the Freedom Frequency

How frequently do you feel free from negative thoughts and emotions? How frequently do you feel happiness or joy during your day?

I have defined the Freedom Frequency as a field of higher "vibrations that consists" of positive emotions or states of higher mind that we experience or want to experience more of, such as peace, trust, happiness, respect, fulfillment, and so on.

The Freedom Frequency is your natural state of being where you experience a higher love for yourself and life. It is here you experience compassion and bring joy to others because you feel it in your heart. It is here that ecstasy goes beyond the orgasm, as we feel the force of the Divine vibrating through every cell of our being.

Being present with where you are right here, right now, with what you *feel* and then sitting in and breathing through the energy that is alive inside of you is where your power is. It is here that you connect to your health and to prosperity consciousness. This is where you truly feel the greatest power in the universe—*Love*. This force is found in the heart center and is only activated through your willingness to connect to Source—your I AM presence. This activation will then revive cellular memory within your entire physical body.

The core essence of the Freedom Frequency is *love*. It is a *higher love*, which I refer to as *enlightened love*. Enlightened love is a direct experience of the Divine. You may experience a moment of this *higher vibrational love* as you embark on your spiritual journey., The more you engage in these moments, the sweetness of this love will become a driving force to experience higher states of being. When you experience *enlightened love*, you will know beyond doubt that there is more to life than meets the eye. As polarity dissolves you will remember you are one with life.

Love, in itself, vibrates at a very high frequency, and as much as you crave the experience of love, you may often hide from it. Only when you are bold enough to make the journey through the frequency of fear (below the line emotional energies) can your physical body resonate in the *enlightened love* vibration.

If you are ready to experience more fulfilling and meaningful relationships and feel wonderful about who you are, then the journey begins with transforming yourself at a foundational level, at a vibratory level. This transformation requires relinquishing the darker forces (*your fears*) that hold you back, so you can spiral up into the lighter energies of love and freedom.

You are here on this planet to do whatever it takes to receive and embrace the energies that vibrate in the *Freedom Frequency*. These higher vibrations are not outside of you. They live within every cell of your physical body.

Today's Higher Idea: Discover what makes you *feel happy and joyful!* Write your Freedom List of twenty-five activities you love to do or want to experience and then imagine yourself doing these things and feeling good about who you are.

Higher Idea #6 You Are Not Your Fear

I have defined the Fear Frequency as energy vibrations that prevent you from completely accessing the higher vibrations in the Freedom Frequency. In other words, the Fear Frequency consists of all the negative emotions, thoughts, and behaviors, such as blame, anger, hate, guilt, worry, anxiety, depression, and so on. This family of lower thought vibrations creates resistance and forgetfulness and can stop you from living your full potential.

Fear is associated with the *ego*, the *"persona,"* the part of you that believes you need to be protected from the illusionary saber-tooth tiger just around the corner. Your ego is an out-dated operating system that has had eons of programming and still believes you are in constant danger. Its only objective is to keep you living in smallness, lack, and limitation. Your *"persona" is a false identity,* and it does *not* want you to jump outside your comfort zone and evolve spirituality. The *ego* is connected to a fear-based mind-control system that has created *false beliefs* about who you are and your reality. When it feels threatened, it will send a signal to your brain, causing the *flight, fight, or freeze* reaction. Your *ego* will resist change at any cost and will do its best to have you remain living in fear. The *ego* is not inherently bad or wrong. It does serve a purpose. However, if you allow your *ego* to *control* you, it can paralyze your dreams, destroy your relationships, debilitate your health, and keep you from being the free sovereign man/woman you are.

Fear is a great teacher because it reminds you to move cautiously so you may embrace the fullness of every experience. However, you are not meant to *live* in the Fear Frequency. Fear is not who you *are*.

The energy of fear is expressed with an array of perceived negative thoughts and images. If your mind shows you painful images of the past, the emotions attached to those memories can have you feeling as if the same traumatic event is happening right now. It is up to us as seekers of self-empowerment to change our idea of what fear is by shifting our perceptions of the past.

Any type of growth will be uncomfortable because it means you are stepping outside your comfort zone, outside the walls of your limited beliefs—and your ego will do anything to avoid feeling uncomfortable. If you stay in this *fear frequency* your physical body will pay the price as the energy of health and wellness does not resonate here.

Today's Higher Idea: What does fear mean to you and how has it held you back in your life? Challenge yourself to step to the edge of your comfort zone. Breathe in the uncomfortable energy. Just breathe.

Higher Idea #7 You Are the Creator of Your Life

What if you discovered that YOU are more powerful than the physical world? What if you discovered that you have an internal universe that is much more powerful than anything outside of you? If this is true, do you think it would be a higher idea to get to know how the power within you is activated?

You are the creator of your own reality. How? By what you choose to *think, feel,* and *believe.* Yes, your thoughts and emotions, whether positive or negative, create your reality. This is how powerful you are. You are creating your reality in the same way others are creating theirs. Yes, every event, situation, or experience you have had, whether good, bad, ugly, or joyful, was created to assist you in waking up to your true power.

It took me a long time to integrate this truth, the truth that I create my experiences by what I choose to believe, think, and feel. In fact, the concept created significant resistance in me because my *ego* wanted to keep me in victim mode. After all, how could I have created all the bad stuff that had happened to me? Others are to blame, right? Should they not be responsible for all the bad things that have happened to me? I discovered the answer was simply, "No!" This meant I could no longer blame anyone for my negative emotions. I could no longer blame the government, God, my parents, my past boyfriends, or anyone else for how I was feeling in the moment.

Really? Yes! And I could no longer blame myself. When I embraced this truth, I began to resonate with the word *accountability*.

Accountability is being fully responsible for your thoughts, words, actions, and experiences without blame, shame, or guilt. You see everything as a process of self-discovery and of remembering your truth. You are on the path to self-governance.

In every moment, your mind is projecting the hologram of your experience through the mental images that are emotionally charged. This is why it is so important to become aware of your thoughts and feelings, and which frequency you are transmitting from—*fear or freedom?* Of course, you are not able to become aware of every thought; after all, you have approximately 70,000 thoughts a day. All you are asked to do is become aware of the thoughts that disempower you or the unkind and unloving thoughts you have about yourself or others and begin at once to exchange these lower ideas into new empowered truths. As you do, you start the process of shifting from your fear-based mind and align with your Divine Mind.

Eastern philosophy reminds us that we live in a thought-powered and feeling-centered universe, which means that whatever emotionally charged thoughts you have will eventually manifest in your life. Thoughts that are emotionally charged from below the line (negatively charged) are fragmented and will create stress, worry, and frustration. Then you wonder why you are having a bad day. Thoughts that resonate from above the line (positively charged) are centered in truth and will create more of the joy, inner peace, and love that you may be seeking.

You are being called to rise up out of the illusory worlds of pain and suffering into worlds of love and freedom. How? By acknowledging and releasing *negative beliefs* that are in the way of creating a life of freedom.

You can get stuck in your day-to-day dramas and think that your present situation is all there is to life; however, there is much more to this reality than meets the eye. This universe is highly intelligent and filled with infinite energy that you are breathing in every second. It is not just air you breathe, it is life-force energy that is forever expanding, renewing, transforming, and creating.

Begin today to see yourself as a Creator of your own life. If you are unhappy, begin projecting out a new hologram of mental images that make you feel happy. See every day as a new day to begin again. Focus on creating this day to teach you more about yourself. When your thoughts are vibrating at higher frequencies, you spiral up into greater experiences of life. Creating a solid foundation in the *Freedom Frequency* requires you to expand your awareness of who you are—the Creator of your life.

Today's Higher Idea: The universe is always expressing through you. What is ready to be expressed through you? What bold actions steps are you ready to take today to make this world a better place? Put your hand to your heart and repeat out loud, "I am the creator of my life."

Higher Idea #8 Choose Where You Want to Vibrate

One of the most powerful questions you can ask yourself every day is, "Where am I vibrating right now, in *fear* or *freedom*?"

The emotions or states of mind in The *Freedom Frequency* Chart (Higher Idea #4) are ones to which we can all relate. There are many more positive or perceived negative emotions or qualities than the ones I listed. This chart is to be used as a reference for the emotionally charged vibrations you may experience throughout your life.

Each positive or perceived negative emotion or state defines a rate of vibration, a level of consciousness that determines how you will think and behave. If you are interested in knowing the exact rate of vibrations, I suggest reading Dr. David R. Hawkins' book, <u>Power vs. Force</u>. Hawkins developed a map of the different levels of consciousness, also known as the Emotional Scale. For example, *shame* vibrates at a frequency of 20 (lower consciousness), which is the lowest on the scale, while *enlightenment* is the highest at 700+ (higher consciousness).

Many of us move in and out of various vibrations and, in doing so, we experience the contrasts of reality. We are all here to experience the lower vibrations contained in the Fear Frequency. However, we are not meant to live here. We are meant to spiral up, to evolve, and to embody the higher vibrations experienced in the Freedom Frequency. This doesn't mean you are to ignore or suppress your negative emotions. In fact, the only way to spiral up is to *feel* everything that is ALIVE inside of you, all *emotions,* without making them wrong, right, good, or bad. I will share powerful practices in the following chapters to assist you.

We have all experienced the emotional roller-coaster of pain and pleasure. Our earthly experience allows us to explore all the energy available to us. Many of us move up and down the scale from the low-energy fields of separation and lack, and then we move up to experience the high-energy fields of joy and alignment with our soul within the frequency of freedom. What many of us discover is that we do not know how to handle the high-energy vibrations contained in the Freedom Frequency for an extended period of time, because we are uncomfortable with the intensity and the power it brings.

Do you remember a moment when you were blissfully happy and then a voice within said, "I wonder how long this will last?" With that doubting thought, you spiral down once more, riding the roller-coaster into the frequency of fear. How long do you stay there? Until you take back your power and remember the *light* within. You stay in this lower vibration until you learn to recognize the gift of your present experience.

The greatest illusion many of us hold is the illusion that the physical world is more powerful than we are. As I mentioned earlier, one of the biggest secrets is that your internal universe (emotional, mental, and spiritual) is much more powerful than anything outside of you. It is a higher idea to begin now and turn your attention inward and explore this inner universe. Let go of allowing the media or outside forces to dictate what you should believe or think.

The key to living above the line is Self-Awareness. Becoming self-aware is observing where your thoughts and emotions take you. Self-Awareness leads to being Self-Directive, directing yourself to live and experience the highest version of you. Learning to direct your thoughts and emotions is realized by observing the fear-based energy and love-based energy that is moving through you, without judging it as good or bad. Becoming an observer of yourself, of your personality (the voices in your head) and not taking it all to heart, leads to feeling whole and complete.

There is a powerful technique I created called the *Divine Mind Conversation* (Chapter Seven), where you learn how to be in the energy of your Divine Mind—the unified field of intelligence—and integrate all *fear-based* energy with *Enlightened Love* energy. In other words, you are bringing your ego and soul into divine union. When the idea of separation or the power struggle in your mind is dissolved, you are on your way to becoming whole and complete as a divine being.

Through the process of education and expanding *self-awareness*, you can gain the knowledge and insights to uplift your life. As your awareness expands and your inner worlds open up, you begin to embrace the realm of *remembering* who you are.

Today's Higher Idea: One of the most powerful questions you can ask yourself is, "Where am I energetically vibrating right now, *fear* or *freedom*?" You are the only one who can consciously choose which frequency you will live in.

Higher Idea #9 Get Real with Where You Are

In order to spiral up in life and live above the line, you will be required to get real with where you are right now. Get real with where you are financially, in your relationships, your environment, your health, your spirituality, your family, and how you feel about your career. This means defining for yourself what you want, what you need, what you believe in, what is important to you, and what your heart desires. In order to know where you want to go in life, you first need to know where you are at.

Facing reality will feel uncomfortable. Why? Because for the most part we do not like looking at ourselves. For instance, some of us would rather avoid opening our bills because we fear we won't have enough money to pay them. Or, some married couples will sleep with their daughters and sons to avoid intimacy with a spouse. Or, we will avoid a daily meditation practice because we are fearful of our own minds.

The more you face the truth and admit to what is present in your life, the more clarity you have around what is working and what is not. Only then can you say, "I have had enough of living this way." Nobody can do this for you. Stop waiting. You are not a follower. You are a leader of your own life, and as you rise up you will feel uncomfortable in the energy of vulnerability. Every empowered or enlightened woman or man has had to move through the *uncomfortableness* (feeling the energy of fear or intense resistance) to become who they are today. Some refer to it as crossing the *universal challenge line* or *rebirthing zone*.

Confusion, chaos, and stress lessen dramatically when you get real with where you are at and face the truth of what *is*. Now, the energy of clarity, focus, direction, and soul-inspired action can spiral you up into living the life your heart desires. You are meant to be happy.

Happiness is realized when you ground yourself in truth, in your own spirituality. Happiness is a truth that can shift your life in very profound ways. Happiness is remembering that nothing in this world is solid or unchanging because your thoughts and emotions are made of energy, and energy is constantly moving. For example, you may be angry with your partner because you feel he/she does not listen to your request for more respect and therefore you avoid him/her. Instead, if you both sat down and expressed, in a healthy way, how this experience may have reminded you of when you were a girl or boy and no one listened to you, then you pop the bubble of blame and projections.

This truth releases pent up negative emotions that have been suppressed, and allows for a healing to take place and your vibration to shift dramatically.

Topics that cause you to feel vulnerable are the exact topics you need to be having conversations about. When you admit and acknowledge your dissatisfaction with your present experience, not from a place of continuous complaint or blame, but facing the truth of how you *feel*, you allow the negative energetic charge you have around your experience to be released.

All the uncomfortable or painful feelings you have about life's issues can eventually transform into curiosity and interest. You are that powerful. Your thoughts and emotions are constantly changing. You can feel depression one moment and enlightenment in the next.

Get real with *what is,* then accept *what is,* and allow life to unfold naturally. The universe knows what you need to heal and will create scenarios for this to occur. As you say, "Yes" to facing each moment, becoming present with your thoughts and feelings, and expressing your truth, your life will start to shift and spiral up.

Creating a solid foundation for your life involves knowing what you believe in, what you stand for, what is important to you, or what you value the most. If you want to experience freedom, you will be asked to step into and acknowledge your present reality.

Today's Higher Idea: Let today be your starting point. Take a moment and write where you're at in your relationship, your career, your finances, your family, and your health. Write about what you do not like and what you will no longer tolerate. You are where you are because of the choices you have made. Now clarify what you want to experience in each life area. Do not edit your thoughts. Write! Write! Write!

Higher Idea #10 Shift Your Perception

The reality you experience is perceptual, meaning everything is based on how you interpret life events. Your view of life depends greatly upon the experiences you had growing up, which then created beliefs about who you think you are.

As you mature, your perceptions evolve in how you view yourself, others, and your life. For example, if you are a woman and perceive men as emotionally unavailable, then that is what you will experience. If you are a man and you view women as gold diggers, then you will attract that kind of woman. If you perceive the world you live in as unsafe or dangerous, then you will not feel safe or supported, no matter what you do. If your perception of your mother or father is negative, then your experience with your mother or father will not be pleasant.

Some of us have experienced so much pain that we choose to live a life with walls around our hearts and minds. What we do not realize is that the emotional and mental pain we hold on to can be transformed and released by shifting our perceptions of our past experiences.

Perceiving your reality from a spiritual or higher perspective brings incredible freedom. For example, in moments where I felt unloved or unappreciated, I soon realized that how I was feeling had nothing to do with anyone else. Turning my attention inward, I could see that I was the one who was not loving or appreciating myself. I was not loving or nurturing my own soul. Everyone outside of me was just a reflection of my own lack of *self-love*. The journey to love began with me.

Viewing yourself and others from a place of love and gratitude brings ultimate freedom. Be patient.

Today's Higher Idea: If you were to sit on a cloud and view your life from above, from a higher vantage point, what changes would you make in how you behave with others? A shift in perception goes a long way.

Higher Idea #11 Benefits of Raising Your Vibration

As women and men, we are motivated in one of two ways. We are either moving away from pain or moving toward pleasure. Every day, we are being sold a product or a service that will help us escape the pain of life or create more pleasure in our lives. The motivation to buy anything comes from knowing how it will benefit our lives.

One of the greatest benefits of raising your vibration from a fear-based consciousness to a love-based consciousness is that you will never feel *lonely* again. Guaranteed! When the energy in your body is vibrating in freedom, you will automatically feel connected to all of life, to the Source of All That Is.

I discovered for myself, when my energy vibration was above the line in the Freedom Frequency, illness became less frequent. The vibration of health is your natural state where energy *flows* through your body with ease.

Another amazing benefit is that you will never have to go looking for love ever again! That's right! It is all right here now! As you open to the Divine love that lives in every cell of your physical body, and consciously expand this vibration out through your heart, you become an attraction magnet drawing others, resources, and whatever you desire into your reality.

Raising your energy vibration will bring the joy, the love, and all the delicious qualities of life into your field of experience. If you do not know how to shift your vibration, keep reading. It is obvious that you are a ready student. This willingness to learn and know the truth about the power that lies inside you is benefiting your life right now.

By raising your vibration, you will know that you are always safe. If you don't feel safe, you are energetically below the line, you lack trust. Trust must be cultivated from within in order to spiral up. As you raise your vibration you begin to trust in yourself as you possess the knowledge and certainty that the journey you are on is divinely perfect. When you send out the vibration of love and gratitude to the earth and all those who live on it, life will support you, Mother Earth will support you, and those you have never met will support you.

If you feel uncertain about what steps to take, this book is intended to remind you to spiral up through your fear, your doubt, and your pain into a higher love and acceptance for who you really are. When you are feeling vulnerable, this is a sign that you are on the right track.

As you raise your vibration, you enter higher states of consciousness, which means you are rising above the fear that consumes many. Living above the line, you embody the higher vibrations of life and will no longer be affected by the negative behaviors or reactions of others. You will see that the only reason we behave negatively is because we are in fear.

The purpose of this journey on earth is for you to remember who you are and to discover that you are much more than what your physical eyes can see. As you spiral up and lighten up your energy vibration and have a more positive outlook on life, you will begin to see more than what you do now. You will have more energy to do what you need to do. You will look and feel younger, without the aid of drugs or surgery, because you are living in the present moment. You will feel a sense of peace within your mind where nothing really bothers you anymore. You will be more accepting of others and who you are. Everything that used to affect you in a negative way no longer will. You will feel a stronger connection with your family and oneness with the world. You will create things and do things you never thought you could before. And the only food, drink, or clothes you will want *in* or *on* your body are high quality. The higher you vibrate the more you raise your standards and your *deserve-ability* factor.

As you raise your energetic vibration from being negatively charged to positively charged, you realize that all the negative thoughts and voices in your head have vanished. You now have one voice, the voice of wisdom, the voice of your Brilliant Self to guide you through life's moments with ease and grace.

There are many incredible benefits when you raise your vibration including being happy for no reason.

Today's Higher Idea: Shifting your vibration means that life as you know it, will change. Any time you feel confused, want to give up, or are frustrated about the journey you are on, remember the benefits of shifting your vibration.

Higher Idea #12 You Always Have a Choice

You have a choice in what you choose to focus on, what you choose to express, and the life you choose to create. You have a choice to think negatively or positively about your life experiences. You have a choice either to say, "Yes" or "No." Your life is made up of choices, and if you do not like what you are creating, then it may be time to make a different choice.

One thing is certain: life will always throw issues, problems, or challenges your way because that is how you discover what you're made of and who you are. The trick is in knowing how to deal with life's challenges and how to overcome fear. You now have a choice to begin viewing all challenges as opportunities to learn about yourself.

You also have the choice to think different thoughts about those in your life. You can choose to see them as divine messengers who are only in your life to remind you of how you see yourself. By making healthier choices based on your values, you lift your life up and attract others of value. You can gain a better understanding of where you are in life by recognizing what frequency zone you are working from— *fear* or *freedom?*

Expanding your awareness of the power that lives inside of you offers you a choice to learn from love instead of riding the roller-coaster into the lower vibrations of chaos, struggle, and suffering in order to learn your life lessons. This does not mean the chaos will end. However, if the seed of chaos no longer lives inside of you, then the chaos created by others will simply become scenery on your ride to living above the line.

Moving out of the *fear frequency* is about *light*ening up! You can choose the feeling of freedom any time by anchoring lighter energies of love, joy, trust, and understanding into your thoughts on a continuous basis. You also have a choice to let go of eating heavy, processed, fear-injected food, and spiral up into eating food that carries life-force energy (*light*) such as fruits and vegetables.

Today's Higher Idea: Demand more from yourself and say, "I choose to feel happiness today." "I choose to make someone smile today." "I choose to say the words, *I love you* and *I am sorry.*"

Higher Idea #13 Commitment Request

Only when you are committed to a higher vision or a higher idea of who you are and what you want your life to be can the universe work its magic. When you sit on the fence of life you are resisting your soul purpose. You are in resistance to your inner brilliance, the gifts within. Breathe in the vibration of trust and courage to no longer resist life. Recommit to the vision within your heart even though you may have no idea where your feet are going to land. As you take the step, the universe works to align you with this new reality. Take a moment now and commit to "Being" who you are here to be. Make your commitment to evolve because you see the intelligence behind it.

State the following out loud:

- I now commit to being flexible and accepting change as a part of life.
- I now commit to discovering the truth of who I am.
- I now commit to relinquishing all lower thoughts and negative ideas that do not serve me.
- I now breathe in the gifts of trust and acceptance.
- I now choose to remember my own value.
- I now commit to understanding my reality and my purpose in it.
- I now commit to remembering my Divine perfection, my greatness, my beauty, and my truth.

- I now commit to deepening my spiritual practice and living in truth.
- I am now committing to reading The Freedom Frequency from front to back and completing every exercise, as it will benefit my life.

So it is!

Chapter Two
Emotional Evolution

Women and men are on the cusp of an emotional evolution. I define emotional evolution as the development from primal emotions (fear) to authentic emotions (love). As we take this evolutionary journey, which involves both emotional intelligence and emotional maturity, we then have the ability to control our lower, fear-based emotional states and align with who we really are as a magnificent Divine being.

We are now embracing higher ideas and becoming accountable for the energy that moves through us. We are on the path to ending the blame game and becoming accountable for how we choose to *feel*.

In this chapter, we will explore your emotions as an intelligent energy that is alive inside of you. I will offer you a powerful new way to view your emotions and an understanding of how they can serve you. For instance, viewing your emotions from a higher perspective will greatly benefit you. How? By viewing emotion as *energy that is alive inside of you.* All energy is intelligence seeking to be experienced through you. When you no longer fear this energy and instead seek to observe it from a place of neutrality, you discover the essence of your true power.

When you shift into observer mode you take your power back because you are no longer having your emotions define you. This doesn't mean ignoring how you feel; in fact, you will embrace how you feel more than ever. As you spiral up in higher states of consciousness, the polarity of good and bad, negative and positive begins to dissolve. What I mean is, you no longer see negative emotions as bad or wrong and positive emotions as good and right. You begin to realize that your emotions are either fear-based or love-based. Your fear-based emotions (the perceived negative emotions) offer you the opportunity to learn about yourself and how you perceive the world around you.

Now you may be wondering why you need to focus on your emotions. How you feel is important. Your emotions are rooted in your beliefs and how you feel will lead to actions and those actions create results. Are you getting the results you desire?

Exploring and learning how to work with your emotional dimension will have a powerful and positive impact on all your relationships, your career, and life experience. The inner work involved may be challenging, time-consuming, and require great patience; however, the rewards are worth it.

Higher Idea #14 Emotional Integrity

Do you believe that emotions represent weakness? Do you do whatever it takes to hide the heavy burden you are carrying? Do you hide behind drugs, alcohol, sex, food, or your career so you won't have to *feel*? Will you do anything to escape *feeling*? The incredible thing about life is that it always forces us to change our limited ideas, and if we continue to ignore the natural laws of creation, the cycle of destruction, tragedy or death is sure to remind us.

Many of us have lost employment, relationships, or connections with family or friends because we don't know how to deal with our emotions. Others stay emotionally distant because they have difficulty managing the complexity of feelings, decisions, and conflicting energies. If we want to improve the quality of our life, knowing how to work with our emotional dimension will assist in building self-esteem and the confidence to handle any situation. We no longer need to buy into the fear and doubt that once paralyzed us.

Emotional Integrity is developing a higher level of awareness that we are only responsible for how we feel, and we are not responsible for how others feel. Emotional Integrity involves accountability, inner strength, and discipline of thoughts. The benefit of Emotional Integrity is that you will no longer be affected in a negative way by what others say or do.

Emotional Integrity is the ability to recognize the truth behind your feelings. If you are unable to manifest what you want in life, it's because you have yet to clear out fear-based energies (limiting beliefs) from your subconscious mind.

You can rise above your pain when you discover the *seed* of your emotions and explore the truth of what you are feeling. You have the power to release heavy energies trapped in your physical body and exchange them for lighter energies that can spiral you up to live above the line. This does not mean creating an emotional scene in order to get your way or to manipulate someone. This pattern will only give you more of what you *don't* want. You are here to release your *fear* of the energy that moves through you.

Every woman or man has both masculine and feminine energies moving through his or her physical body. Our masculine qualities represent the leader within, the one who is action-orientated, strategizes, and protects while our feminine qualities mirror that of the nurturer, the receiver, and the flow of emotions. Allowing these energies to be expressed in a balanced and healthy way is essential to our spiritual and emotional evolution.

An extreme shift within men and women has taken place over the last two decades. Women, who were once extremely emotional, have now shut down their feeling centers in order to operate in the masculine world of power, control, and action. Women are being guided now to embrace their Divine Feminine and dissolve the closed or guarded hearts they have toward men or the masculine energy within. Thankfully, more men are experiencing a transformation as they embrace their feminine energies within. Where emotions were once avoided, men are now giving themselves permission to feel and allowing tears to flow, dissolving past myths of what courage and strength really mean.

It is only a guarded or closed heart that stops us from experiencing the depth of our own feelings. As women and men embrace a more heart-centered life together, we harmonize the energies of masculine and feminine and have the power to create heaven on earth.

Today's Higher Idea: Free yourself from the idea that emotions are weak and allow for a deeper expression to be realized. Talk to someone you trust about how you feel or take time to write in your journal and express your truth.

Higher Idea #15 Discover Your Guidance System

Do you know the number one cause of a ruined vacation? Or what has the power to ruin a special evening, end a relationship, or a business opportunity? The answer is *destructive negative emotions.*

Since our third dimension is based in polarity, at opposite ends of the spectrum, we experience two main frequencies *fear* and *love (freedom)* and everything in between. One is based in illusion and the other in truth. All emotions, positive and negative, vibrate within the range of these two main frequencies.

From this point forward, I recommend you view your emotions as your internal guidance system. If you are feeling uncomfortable in your skin, it means your thoughts are incorrect and you are vibrating in the Fear Frequency. If you are feeling happy about yourself and your life, it means your thoughts are in alignment with truth and you are vibrating in the Freedom Frequency. For example, if you are feeling stressed (below the line), your body is telling you to stop what you are doing and find a quiet place to meditate so you can shift your vibration. When you are stressed, your mind is in overwhelm and cannot come up with a solution. You will benefit greatly the more you tune in and listen to your body.

Yoga is another powerful gift you can give yourself as it will reduce the tension buildup and you will learn how to ground yourself and *be* in your body.

Emotion is *energy in motion,* and this energy flows through every cell of your physical body. Listening to your inner guidance system means tuning in to how you feel in your body in the present moment. How you feel either represents the vibration of *ease* (above the line) or the vibration of *dis-ease* (below the line). If the energy in your body is negatively charged (not in ease), then you are being reminded to stop what you are doing, meditate, and contemplate a different course of action that speaks to your heart.

Today's Higher Idea: Your fear-based emotions are like red flags, warning you about the thoughts you are having. Practice non-judgment of these emotions when they arise. Could your thoughts or perceptions be incorrect about the situation? Where is your mind directing you—*fear or freedom?* Get *real* with how you *feel* so you can let the lower energies of fear move through you.

Higher Idea #16 Your Emotions are Liquid Energy

Emotions are the same for everyone. Throughout our lives we all experience the roller-coaster of perceived positive and negative emotions. The only difference is the degree to which we allow perceived negative emotions to take us down into the lower realms of fear and consume our lives.

Are you willing to connect to your Courageous Self and explore the depths of your subconscious— the feeling center of your being? In order to progress mentally, emotionally, spiritually, and physically, you will be required to acknowledge and be present with any fear-based energy that has been holding you back. We will explore the other phases of mind in Chapter Three, because it is the invisible aspects of who you are that hold the key to lasting transformation.

Your mind can become attached to others, ideas, things, or events, and it is your emotional attachments and how you interact with others that create the emotional roller-coaster you often experience. Since life is about beginnings and endings or creation and destruction, everyone eventually experiences detachment or loss. You may experience the end of an intimate relationship, death of a loved one, or loss of a job, which can create the feeling of being rejected, unloved, or unsupported.

Your emotional dimension connects you to stored memories in your subconscious mind and the uncomfortable truths attached to unresolved issues. Emotions, positive or negative, create long-term memories, that become locked up in your cells. Whether you have installed pleasant or unpleasant memories within your cells determines how you will perceive the many moments that make up your life. Emotional integrity involves the process of filtering out and transforming the collective lower thought forms (beliefs) from your subconscious mind so you can free yourself from painful memories or your wounded stories and live fully in the present.

It's time to take a closer look at the lower energies that move through your body and how you can learn to control them, so your life integrates with the higher vibrations in the Freedom Frequency.

Viewing your emotions as energy flowing through you like water allows you to step out of *becoming* your negative emotions. This distinction will change your life and profoundly shift how you relate to others. Again, it is important to emphasize here that you will require a certain amount of inner strength to readjust your thinking.

Since you have a desire to live above the line, then all family, financial, self-related, or sexual issues that hold a negative emotional charge will require your attention. This means that every time you are triggered or your buttons are pushed (congratulate the man or woman who has the power to do this as they are divinely here to assist you in achieving emotional maturity), you are being asked to get real with how you feel.

A negative emotional charge with others only leads to lost or missed opportunities that could have brought many gifts. This is why it is important to bring your emotional energy into harmonic balance, and once your negative interactions with others become neutralized, you will have become an empowered Divine being.

Your emotions are constantly changing from one moment to the next. For instance, you can go from a state of sadness and within moments be laughing at your predicament. In one moment you can be angry with your spouse and the next minute your heart is open to love. You connect to your inner power the more you begin to see your emotions as fluid energy flowing through you and constantly changing. You have the power to feel what you want to feel in every moment.

Gregg Braden is a thought leader, bestselling author, speaker, and a brilliant teacher of spiritual science. I have learned much about myself through his work. Here is one of my favourite powerful quotes written by this wise man:

Modern science has discovered that through each emotion we experience in our bodies, we also undergo chemical changes of things such as pH and hormones that mirror our feelings. Through the "positive" experiences of love, compassion, and forgiveness and the "negative" emotions of hate, judgment, and jealousy, we each possess the power to affirm or deny our existence at each moment of every day.

- Gregg Braden

Today's Higher Idea: From the *Freedom Frequency* List in Higher Idea #4, express out loud which states of being you are ready to claim such as, "I AM joy! I AM peace! I AM love!" Claim it! Louder!

Higher Idea #17 See the Gift of Negative Emotions

Viewing my perceived negative emotions as a gift transformed my life completely. Growing up, I used to be so frustrated with my mother and father and their inability to communicate with one another. Their negative interactions and emotional way of being were transferred to me, and I carried their beliefs like a monkey on my back right into my adult life. When I was bored in my relationships, I would stir the pot and create drama by yelling and venting as I had no idea what to do with all the uncomfortable energy inside my body. I played the blame game just like my mother and father had.

Yes, I wore the face of a happy woman when I was out in the world, but in my home, I became a wild woman and had many moments of rage, especially toward the men in my life. Underneath the anger stirred a deep sadness and underneath the sadness were many layers of fear, such as the fear of being misunderstood, fear of abandonment, fear of being unloved, and the fear of rejection. Of course, I was completely unaware that my negative emotions were based in fear. In fact, if you had told me I was living in fear I would have thought you were crazy. I lacked the knowledge and understanding of myself, my emotions, and the truth of my reality.

We are not given a life manual in school or taught how to handle the intense emotional energy that moves through us. I am grateful to have been shown a path to living in internal freedom. It was not an easy journey as my fear-based mind did not want to let go. Devotion and dedication to experiencing *enlightened love* is what got me through the tough times.

As I opened up spiritually and deepened into my practice of daily meditation, I began to see the many invisible and multi-dimensional worlds that made up my life experience. I discovered that changing my perceptions about my emotions was a huge gift.

You have the power to transform the seed of all negative emotions. However, these emotions can only be transformed authentically when you are open to receiving the gift each one brings to your life.

A gift you can give yourself is to remember that you are not your emotions. Emotions are a form of intelligence that wants to be experienced by you. You are not meant to become and be overtaken by emotions. You can only *feel* anger. You can only *feel* jealousy. You can only *feel* sadness. Once you *feel* the emotion fully, which means acknowledging and embracing the energy, you then release it by allowing it to flow through you. How? Keep reading.

All perceived negative emotions remind you that there is something in your life that requires your attention and needs to be resolved. Underneath anger is sadness and underneath sadness is fear. Therefore, we need to get real with ourselves and acknowledge the fear within. Underneath your fear is a power so great – *your Divine Mind.*

Many of us have a difficult time believing we fear anything at all. However, all perceived negative emotions are associated with one or many fears, such as fear of being misunderstood, being wrong, losing control, being alone, not being heard, and so on. Anger, for example, is an obvious reflection of deep dissatisfaction with our life and a desperate yearning for change.

To make this simple, let's imagine a cherry pie filled with one hundred cherries. Each cherry represents an emotion, some being positive and some being negative (experience duality then unity). The totality of who you are is the complete cherry pie. Now, all the positively charged cherries are sweet and yummy and all the negatively charged cherries are sour and poisonous. Your role on earth is to transform all your sour and poisonous cherries into sweet and delicious cherries so you become a Divine cherry pie that attracts everyone who is vibrating in positive resonance. Each of us is expressing from a place of either Divine sweetness or poisonous ego. Not good or bad. It just *IS*.

From this point forward, see yourself having *emotional moments*, not stressful or bad days, or angry weeks or depressing years. Moments!

Today's Higher Idea: If you look at the Freedom Frequency Chart (Higher Idea #4) and add up all the fear-based energies you experience, then you know how many sour and poisonous cherries you are ready to transform into sweet and yummy cherries. What gifts are you willing to see behind any perceived negative emotions you have experienced in the last month?

Higher Idea #18 Only Your Thoughts Make You Feel

At the beginning of this chapter, I stated that we are experiencing an emotional evolution. I defined emotional evolution as *having a higher level of awareness that we are only responsible for how we feel, and we are not responsible for how others feel.*

What did you feel about this statement? Any resistance? Let me clarify. Here is the biggest secret of all. You may want to sit down for this one. Okay, here it is...

Nothing outside of you can make you angry, frustrated, happy, or sad. I know this concept may be difficult to grasp and you may resist the idea at first. The truth is, no one makes you feel *angry,* no one makes you feel *sad,* and no one has the power to make you feel *happy.* No one has the power to make you feel *anything.* It is only your *thoughts* that have that power to make you *feel.* This is how powerful your thoughts and emotions are. Positive thoughts create higher states of energy in your body and negative thoughts create lower states of energy in your body. If you are not feeling well in your body, immediately make a course correction in your thinking and you will begin to feel a subtle shift, a lightening up, in your body. Your thoughts and imagination carry infinite power. This is the path to enlightenment.

When you acknowledge the source of your emotions and realize that how you feel in the moment has nothing to do with anyone outside of yourself, you will be empowered. It is only your thoughts, your beliefs, and the mental images you have *within* you that create your emotions and perceptions of reality. Yes, you may have experienced some horrific moments in your life that caused pain and hurt, and it *is* easier to blame others for what happened in the past. However, as difficult as it may be to admit, nothing *outside* of you is the cause. Your soul is guiding you on a journey to remember who you are.

You are the creator of your life experience. This means you can no longer blame anyone or anything outside of yourself for any of your life experiences. Your *soul* made a contract to come to this planet to open up and remember the *love* that it IS. If you needed to experience drama, trauma, or tragedy to open your heart to love yourself, then all is divinely perfect. You are on a journey of remembering. Yes, this is accountability, or should I say, *soul accountability.*

We have always been resistant to new ideas. Take time to allow this information, this *transformation,* to integrate into every cell of your body. Breathe in this truth! You are being called to live and be fully accountable for everything in your life, including how you *feel.*

Today's Higher Idea: Say to yourself, "I am now accountable for how I feel." Now, instead of saying, "I am angry," you can say, "I feel angry." Instead of saying, "I am frustrated," you can say, "I feel frustrated." Or better yet, "I am feeling fear and I am letting it pass through me as I AM remembering that I AM LOVE."

Higher Idea #19 You Are Not a Victim of Life

Do you have a *Poor Me* story? If you do, it will stop you from raising your vibration and living above the line. Self-pity is a very destructive emotion that will trap you in lower life experiences. Many of us use self-pity as an excuse to be victims. Excuses such as, "He made me do it," or "She makes me so angry" are victim talk. The *Poor Me* self misinterprets life's events as being wrong or bad instead of seeing everything as a learning opportunity to remember Self Love and Enlightened Love for others.

If you let the feeling of being sorry for yourself consume you, you will create more of what you do not want. This is when you need to discipline your fear-based mind and give space to the Empowered Self that says, "I have had enough. I will no longer tolerate this. I am now going to take inspired action and bring more of what I want into my life."

If you have ever wondered why you have those who are negative or manipulative in your life, it is because a deeper part of you resonates with that woman or man. We only associate and bond with those we resonate with—*those who vibrate at the same frequency as we do.* For instance, if you are vibrating in the Fear Frequency, you may feel the emotions of anger, blame, resentment, neglect, abuse, or betrayal. If your thoughts choose to remain bitter, yet you seek relationships, you will only attract others who mirror your unresolved issues.

Victim consciousness is where we blame others for how we feel. If we stay in the victim vibe for too long, we will eventually attract those with a predator consciousness. Why? Because victims and predators vibrate at the same level of consciousness, just like the abused and the abuser. I know because I have been raped and abused. The only way I was going to attract respectful men into my life was first to start respecting and loving myself and to see my body as the temple that housed my soul.

Secondly, I had to make the choice to no longer tolerate such behaviour from anyone. Then I had to change the mental images I carried in my mind because men could only show up in my life with those images of what I believed to be true. I had to change the way I viewed men and come to see that not all men were unkind or uncaring. I chose to believe that I could and would attract only loving, respectful, and kind men into my life, authentic *gentlemen*. Once I made the choice to connect with the higher energies that live above the line, I spiralled up and began to attract others in my life who respected, honoured, and supported my journey.

If you are transmitting desperate or needy energy signals, they are read loud and clear in any environment where you play or work. It is here that you can allow for clarity and ask yourself, "Am I playing the role of a victim?" If you are, give yourself the gift of time to reflect on your invisible dimensions (*emotional, spiritual, and mental*) to help you shift your beliefs and patterns. The neediness is a reflection of a lack of love for yourself. When you stop feeling sorry for yourself and end the game of trying to please others in order to be liked, and begin to see that everything has happened to you for a higher purpose, you will begin to spiral up. Everything in life is designed to take you in one direction, to wake you up, and to help you remember who you are. You are not a victim of life. You are extraordinary beyond belief.

It is also important to release the idea that you need to feel sorry for others. Let go of the idea that you need to pity others. Each divine being is on his or her own journey, and only that man or woman's soul knows what lessons he or she needs to learn. We cannot judge another's choices as wrong, right, good, or bad. It is all perfectly orchestrated, and we are not here to interfere. We can give guidance and send our love, but we need to allow others to make their own choices and respect those choices no matter how we might feel.

The *Pity self* is also one who complains, and a complainer is always dissatisfied with life—that's *fear-based* living. I recommend you make the choice never to complain again and instead to breathe in the energy of gratitude. The vibration of gratitude will spiral you up faster than you can say, *"Freedom Frequency"*.

Today's Higher Idea: Discipline yourself to stop complaining or blaming others for one week. Instead of focusing on the negative behaviours or attitudes of others, focus on adjusting your own thoughts and actions. What can you do to add joy and comfort to those around you? Remember, insecurity speaks loudly.

Higher Idea #20 Meet Your Inner Fallen Angels

We all have an inner dialogue – our inner *self-talk*. Have you ever wondered where the voices you hear in your head come from? What if you discovered that for every perceived negative/ positive emotion or quality you experience, there is *self* that belongs to that voice? Since emotion is energy and energy is divinely intelligent, it would make sense that this intelligence has a voice.

From a spiritual perspective, I see everyone as an Angel here to collectively co-create heaven on earth. When I refer to heaven, I am not referring to heaven in the religious sense, as something out there led by a bearded man in the clouds. I am referring to an earthly experience where we, as divine beings, have all opened our eyes to the truth; the truth that love, peace, beauty, joy, and abundance is here for every soul to experience fully. You are here to create a beautiful life.

Birthing onto this planet, you arrived innocent and connected to Source. As you were growing up, you forgot where you came from and your energy split, allowing the lower energies of third dimensional life to take over. This physical world was created so you could experience yourself as separate from the whole and then make the journey to remembering who you truly are—an *Earth Angel* of love and light. When you see beyond the veils of illusion, you will see that heaven is right here, right now.

If you stay in darkness (forgetfulness) too long, your soul becomes fragmented and each fragmented part becomes attached to negative experiences in your past, thus creating the negative voices you hear in your conscious mind, or the constant negative thoughts rising up from the depths of your subconscious mind.

Controlling your mind and emotions can be challenging. Have you ever raged at someone or lost your mind for a moment? Then you probably wondered how you got so out of control—like a puppet on a string. You may have to ask yourself, "Who is holding the strings?"

You are here to free yourself and cut the strings. How? Keep reading. There are fragmented parts of you that have had many labels such as gremlins, shadow selves, demons of the mind, or dark forces. These names do not create a high level of willingness for us to go in and explore ourselves, so I have chosen to use the name, *Fallen Angel*.

The word angel symbolizes an *angle of light* that has been blocked from reflecting truth. When I imagine a Fallen Angel, I see an angel with a broken wing. Many of us have become angels with broken wings. This perspective allows us to have a deeper level of compassion for ourselves and ignites a willingness to go inward and seek out our own inner Fallen Angels so we can restore and heal those parts of ourselves that we have forgotten. I recommend that you let go of any religious associations of Fallen Angels (outside of you) and instead, focus and connect to your own spirituality (within you). See yourself in a whole new light.

Now, let's look at your emotions from a higher perspective. What if you saw all your perceived negative emotions as your inner *Fallen Angels* who live below the line and all your positive emotions as your inner *Forgotten Angels* who live above the line? What if you are the one who fell from heaven into this third dimension of many Fallen Angels who forgot who they were? You can create hell or wake up and create heaven right here, right now. Your journey on earth involves learning how to transform your inner Fallen Angels (negative beliefs about yourself) and open to your inner Forgotten Angels (empowering beliefs about yourself) so you can integrate more light (truth) and achieve a higher state of consciousness. It is time to "be" the Remembered Angel you are so you can spread your wings and be whole and complete as a Divine woman or man.

Let's take a moment and explore your inner Fallen Angels and what they have to teach you. I believe there is a defining moment in our lives when these Fallen Angels take over our mind, body, and soul, just like what happened to me when I was a teenager. Some of us are aware of this moment while others are not.

Fallen Angels are the storytellers, the voices in your head that make you believe you are not worthy, that you do not deserve goodness, that you will never manifest what you want, that you are not good enough, or do not know enough. Can you relate?

Your Fallen Angels symbolize the fragmented *selves* of your personality, and they live in the Fear Frequency. These inner voices are not yours. They belong to the collective consciousness of all eight billion souls on the planet. You just tune into them when you are allowing your *ego* to run your life.

At the core of the Fear Frequency is your *ego*. The *ego* does not want you to connect to your Forgotten Angels who reside above the line because that is where your power lies.

Your Fallen Angels include the:

- Wounded self who carries the seed of all wounds,
- Guilty self who carries the seed of all your guilt,
- Stressful self who carries the seed of all your stresses,
- Frustrated self who carries the seed of all your frustrations,
- Sad self who carries the seed of all your sadness, and
- Angry self who carries the seed of all your anger.

And the list goes on. If you find yourself stressed, frustrated, or angry too often, the only way to end the cycle of these negative emotions is to turn inward and finally see your *self*, the Fallen Angel within who carries the seed. In this way, you become fully accountable and can no longer blame your job, spouse, family, or outer life for how you feel. This is the true essence of *self-responsibility*—the ability to *respond* rather than *react* to the energy that is alive inside.

Your Fallen Angels will continually tell you stories to keep your vibration in the Fear Frequency so they can survive, control you, manipulate you, and deceive you into actions and behaviours that are unhealthy and do not serve your greater good. Each Fallen Angel is a multi-dimensional aspect of your mind with its own individuality and its own defense system. The Fallen Angels remain in control until you make the conscious choice to take your power back.

There are many internal *selves* among your inner Fallen Angels. However, in the next three Higher Ideas I have highlighted three Fallen Angels—the Guilty self, the Angry self, and the Addictive self. These Fallen Angels (inner demons that somehow got trapped into your energy field) have the ability to damage or destroy relationships...and your dreams.

I created the *Divine Mind Conversation,* which is a powerful way to dissolve any and all negative energy you may have wrapped around your past experiences. Releasing the negative energetic charge you have within your mind and body is the key to raising your vibration and living in the Freedom Frequency. This is a powerful tool to use as you learn how to transform the voices within, unlocking eons of programming and becoming *liberated.*

You will know when the negative energetic charge has been released because you will no longer be triggered or react from a place of fear. You will no longer take anything your Fallen Angels says to heart, and eventually their voices will begin to disappear. The *Divine Mind Conversation* shows you how to become the observer of yourself (the many selves). Once your Fallen Angels no longer affect you in a negative way, you'll open yourself up to the higher vibrations of life. Now you have the ability to ignite, embrace, and illuminate your inner Forgotten Angels (loving energy), which will uplift your life.

Today's Higher Idea: Become aware of the negative voices in your head. Define which ones control you and decide whether you are ready to take your power back.

Higher Idea #21 Release Your Guilty Self

If you have the voice in your head that says, "I should have done this," or "I should have done that," or "I should be more…," or "I should *not* have done that," then you are allowing your Guilty self to take over your life. What if you discovered that everything you have ever said or done was meant to happen for the evolutionary growth of everyone involved?

We all have an internal meter reader, which lets you know how you truly feel about the actions you are taking. Guilty pleasures are actions you believe you should not do, but you do them anyway.

Your Guilty self can drain you emotionally and lower your self-esteem if you let it run your life. Ultimately, your Guilty self can cause regret and shame related to past events in which you believe you may have said, thought, or done wrong. Guilt can also show up if you had intentions and did not take action. The Guilty self is partners with the Procrastinator self, which encourages self-sabotage.

As with every Fallen Angel, there is a gift inside— and the gift your Guilty self offers is to help you remember your values. Your Guilty self will 'red flag' you if your actions are not in alignment with your deepest core values. When you experience guilt, you are criticizing yourself and labelling yourself wrong instead of learning from the experience. With every action you take you are given an opportunity to learn more about yourself. If you do not like the actions you have taken in the past, then you have an opportunity to course correct next time.

Guilt can also stop you from taking necessary and constructive action in the present moment. For example, a mother or father who feels guilty for divorcing her or his spouse. This guilt may cause her or him to be more of a friend to their daughters and sons than follow through with the discipline and guidance they actually need.

Life is about learning, unlearning, and relearning. With every action, you discover what works and what does not. With every behaviour you discover what repels others and what creates connection. With every experience, you open to who you are *not* and who you really *are*.

You have the power to rewrite your past by seeing the gift in all experiences. When you listen to your inner higher guidance, you will do things for others because you *want to* and not because you feel you *have to*. Forgive yourself for who you *were* and focus on who you are *now*. When your behaviour and actions are in alignment with your values, you will release the vibration of guilt. This is a journey and requires much patience. Regret also disappears when you view every moment as a learning opportunity.

As long as you carry the *seed* of guilt, your Guilty self will keep you locked up in the past. It is time to tell your Guilty self you are setting yourself free from resentment, shame, regret, and guilt because you know everything has happened for your highest good. You are now making the choice to take inspired action and align with the higher energies of self-acceptance, self-honour, and self-love.

Remember, all behaviours, no matter if they are bad or good, are to be *expressed* as we open up to the truth of who we are. You are also a divine messenger and everything you did in your past was helping others learn about themselves. For example, if you were mean, cruel, or rude, you were there to remind others of what they are choosing to tolerate. You were also mirroring aspects of themselves they did not love. You also assisted others to say no to toxic attachment, to wake up to their spirituality, or to detach from those who do not respect them. You may have been assisting others in opening their hearts to compassion and understanding. You have no idea how your words, actions, and behaviours were a necessary part of another's evolution, or the catalyst necessary for them to spiral up and raise their vibration into higher worlds of love, support, and connection. These words do not give you permission to be unkind to others. These words are here to help you forgive yourself.

Today's Higher Idea: What if you could let go of the idea that you made any mistakes in the past? What if you discovered that your *God Self* or *Goddess Self* wanted to experience everything through you, just for the sake of experiencing life on earth from one spectrum to the other?

Higher Idea #22 Forgive Your Angry Self

Do you *react* or *respond* to life? We are idea-creating, opinion-forming, and decision-making beings. How you deal with everyday problems and stresses is always up to you. We all have an Angry self, and if we do not acknowledge this inner Fallen Angel it can destroy harmony in any and all relationships. The Angry self is an accumulation of all incorrect thoughts that are locked in a vibration with the physical body and also within the collective consciousness. This self absorbs everything internally and thrives on disrupting peace and connection with others. This self rebels against higher learning.

The Angry self enjoys being right and making everyone wrong. This self also *thrives* on being in control and having power over others by forcing others to listen to its ranting and raving and making sure it is understood…or else! This Fallen Angel is deeply afraid of having a heart-to-heart conversation, and it will sabotage any sign of intimacy as intimacy involves vulnerability and losing control.

The Angry self reacts in frustration and cannot handle the smallest amount of stress. The Angry self has expectations of how others *should* respond or act and when they do not act in the expected way this self reacts. It doesn't take much for something to raise our blood pressure when others don't behave how we think they should. It can be anything from someone cutting us off on the freeway to a simple misunderstanding. We then justify our thoughts in an attempt to explain our reactions. We find reasons for being angry and frustrated, and as long as we are hanging on to the victim story of our past or blaming others for how our life is, we will feel powerless.

This Fallen Angel believes that others are to blame for what has happened to you instead of allowing you to be accountable for your own feelings and experiences. This Fallen Angel is very insecure and constantly creates misunderstandings. I am sure you have noticed yourself go through an irrational set of actions because of an issue that surfaced. It means a memory has been stimulated, causing you to *react* instead of *respond* to a situation.

If your Angry self is constantly lashing out and sabotaging the goodness in your life, it means you have allowed one cherry out of your entire Divine cherry pie to take over. This voice within your mind will always tell you lies, and if you let it, it will turn the smallest issue into the biggest war zone. It is time to reclaim your divine power.

You may be unaware of your behaviour in that moment when a Fallen Angel takes over your mind. This is when you really need to pay attention to it. Every issue you encounter helps you expand your awareness of these inner selves that control you like a puppet. Remember, as long as the Angry self is in control of your life, tragedies or unpleasant situations may arise, forcing you to open your heart and see the truth—*nothing or no one is against you*! It is time to claim your power back so you can see the gifts in all things in life. For within every crisis is a gift—a reason for the experience.

This Fallen Angel has not been taught how to respond to life from an emotionally mature place as it's a reflection of the child within who feels unloved and unappreciated. Yes, your Angry self may direct blame at others in your life, but the truth is, your Angry self is angry with *you* for not living fully and for ignoring your own values, passions, and dreams.

You are on this planet to direct the many *selves* within and begin the journey of integration. When you learn how to listen to what your Fallen Angels need or want from you (*which is self-love*), you'll discover there is light at the end of every tunnel.

To transform an Angry self into a *Remembered Angel* requires awareness, inner reflection, acknowledgment, and a willingness to transform your behaviour. I will share more in upcoming chapters on how to deepen into greater *self-love* for all the Fallen Angels alive inside of you.

All perceived negative emotions represent a lack of self-love, self-worth, self-forgiveness, and self-respect. You are being called right now to become self-responsible for how you feel without guilt, shame, or blame. When this happens, your world will transform completely.

Today's Higher Idea: When you feel anger, you are really only ever angry with yourself. Always apologize for venting and spewing toxic energy on the ones you love, and follow through with acts of kindness. The *Divine Mind Conversation* (Higher Idea #79) is a powerful way to release your anger.

Higher Idea #23 Say Goodbye to Your Addictive Self

Addiction has become a rampant illness. Since I am not a doctor or psychologist, I can only share my own experience of how I allowed my Addictive self to control my life. In this book's introduction, I shared how I suffered with drug and alcohol addictions in my early twenties. I felt so alone and the only way I felt connected or had any sense of belonging was in the company of those who liked to party non-stop. It was in this world of toxicity that I felt invincible.

Although many organizations and programs are available to aid in transforming these addictions, I engaged in my own self-healing. With self-discipline and devotion to my own soul, I journeyed within and began the process of aligning with my Divine Mind and communicating with my Addictive self, who had really taken over the Divine cherry pie of my life. My Addictive self felt empty, was very needy, and was always seeking unhealthy ways to fill up the void. This Fallen Angel created a belief within me that I needed cigarettes, alcohol, and drugs to feel *something* other than the emotional pain I had buried deep inside. I did not know how to feel happy naturally.

The Addictive self believes that the only way to move through a life of hell, chaos, struggle, pain, and loneliness or to feel a sense of control, is with a man-made product such as coffee, cigarettes, refined sugar, processed food, drugs, or alcohol. This *self* will have you believe that one of these substances will make the emotional and mental pain go away. Sometimes it might, but only temporarily.

If the Addictive self remains in control, it can destroy lives, businesses, your health, and relationships. In an intimate relationship, it can drive you away from your beloved and into a fantasy world of pornography and sexual affairs.

The Addictive self will use your imagination against you, creating a reality within your mind that is untrue. It will have you believe in the craziest ideas that go against your values. Meanwhile, so long as the Addictive self remains in control, your soul, your divine essence, is being locked up in an inner prison cell.

Give yourself a gift and let go of the idea that you need to grasp obsessively at something external (human-made) to feel *full!* The fullness you seek is spiritual fulfillment. When you face your Addictive self and discover the truth that all this *self* craves is your LOVE, self-love, you'll realize that your cravings have nothing to do with what is outside of your body. Self-love is all any of your Fallen Angels crave. It is your acknowledgment that they exist that will turn your life around. Turn your focus to the knowledge that your Divine nature is calling and that you have an extraordinary inner power to transform your life, and you will turn all the mental and emotional pain into the peace and happiness you seek. You have legions of angels waiting to assist you through your darkest times.

You are here to enjoy and experience everything! We are here to eat and enjoy chocolate, great sex, money, and all the things that give us pleasure. At the same time, we need to stay centered in our power as Divine beings. We are to obtain self-mastery within the physical world—not to be controlled by it.

Today's Higher Idea: Ask yourself, "Do I control what goes into my body? Am I allowing processed human-made products such as tobacco, alcohol, or food to control me? If I am on the path to loving myself, is what I am doing to my body a reflection of that love?"

Higher Idea #24 Remember Your Inner Forgotten Angels

I have defined what your Fallen Angels are. Now, let's take a look at your inner Forgotten Angels more fully. Your Forgotten Angels represent your authentic emotions or higher states of mind, such as love, joy, bliss, happiness, purpose, health, and all the higher vibrations of energy that live above the line in the *Freedom Frequency* Chart (Higher Idea #4).

Our Forgotten Angels carry Divine intelligence, and I refer to them as the Forgotten Angels because these are aspects of ourselves that we have forgotten. Even though we are Divine beings, we have forgotten our Divine nature. We have forgotten that happiness, passion, bliss, abundance, health, and love *is* our natural state of being. Every desirable state or quality lives inside of us…and it is up to us to remember.

To connect with your Forgotten Angels, I suggest you visualize them as higher versions of who you are, such as: your Brilliant Self, your Loving Self, your Joyful Self, your Godman Self, your Goddess Self, your Wise Self, your Passionate Self, Your Healthy Self, and so on. You get the higher idea here, right?

You may have noticed that I use an uppercase 'Self' when referring to a Forgotten Angel such as your Brilliant *Self* and I use a lowercase 'self' when referring to your Fallen Angels such as your Angry *self*. Upper and lower says it all.

Okay, moving on. It's time to dive in and discover the secrets of your spiritual dimension. When expanding your perceptions about who you are and what your true reality is, you may experience resistance. All resistance: fear, darkness, and ego are associated with your Fallen Angels who reside below the line. Acceptance, love, light, and soul are associated with your Forgotten Angels who energetically vibrate above the line.

Your Forgotten Angels carry the seeds of appreciation, joy, love, and respect which are required to create the fulfilling relationship you seek. For instance, once you connect to your Joyful Self, you will want to bring more joy into your beloved's experience. When you connect to your Happy Self, you will naturally have a desire to bring happiness into your relationship. You will remember the joyful and happy man or woman your beloved once was and the joyful and happy *soul* you once were. This is the path to restoring the love you once had. As you focus more on the good and why you embraced love with each other in the first place, you will attract and experience more of the good that has always been there.

Your Forgotten Angels will also assist you in your business. I have imagined my Forgotten Angels, like the Knights of the Round Table, are here to serve for the highest good of all. I have visualized them to be my *inner* Board of Directors, who offer insights and higher perspectives. Through this creative visualization process, I have received profound information that has guided me and my business to where I am today.

When you acknowledge and integrate these Forgotten Angels who carry higher thought forms of information, they will assist you in transforming your Fallen Angels and help you take back your power as a Divine human being.

Today's Higher Idea: Write a list of what makes your *beloved* joyful. If you don't know, *ask*. Write a list of what makes you happy. Now share your lists and take steps that create laughter, joy, and peace even when you don't want to. Heart-centered actions create a smile and have the power to take you to a new level of being together.

Higher Idea #25 Embrace Your Tears

Emotional Integrity is about being fully present and accountable for how you feel, in all ways.

Have you been afraid to feel the energy that is ALIVE inside of you? When was the last time you allowed yourself to *cry* fully? I mean really allowed yourself the time and space to *sob* until you experienced a place of inner peace?

With all life losses, there is a grieving process. Unfortunately, many of us have been taught to avoid the grieving process, so all these hurtful feelings are deposited into the subconscious mind with the hope that they will be forgotten. If we continue to ignore our feelings, the suppression of these heavy energies within the body will eventually explode in anger or rage, causing external destruction in our relationships and/or put the body in a state of *dis-ease*. Emotions do not have to overwhelm us if we make the healthy choice to honour how we feel in every moment.

When the pain of life is so intense, you may want to shut down completely. I am asking you to resist the urge to do so. This does not mean you have to relive each hurtful experience. In order for any emotional pain to be transformed, you need to shift through your resistance and allow the full expression of your emotional pain to be acknowledged in a healthy way. I am here to assist you in learning how to let go through the transformative power of *tears*.

Tears are the most powerful cleansing mechanism your physical body has. Accepting your feelings is a huge step in taking your power back. Tears offer the space to shift your beliefs and create new empowering choices. Ultimately, tears strengthen your inner core as they cleanse your memory banks of all stored experiences that hold a negative energetic charge linked to your past.

Everything that is not built on truth will eventually collapse. Tears are the crumbling of an illusion, the grieving of a perceived loss. On the other side of tears is where you recognize the truth of who you are, your own Divine nature.

Your emotions carry important information, and if you do not listen to the energies that move through you, you may take a path that will not serve your highest good. Allowing your emotions to be experienced as energy moving through you without judging the sensation as wrong or right, good or bad, brings forth your wisdom and opens up the prison gates. Trapped energy in your body can be released through the natural and transformative process of *tears*.

Have you ever cried and afterward felt depressed and lost? Now you can learn how to free your tears and, at the same time, feel empowered on the other side of those tears. Underneath your anger, sadness, and fear is your Divinity. The only reason you are angry, sad, or fearful is because you have forgotten the light, the connection to Source that lives inside of you.

To be an empowered being, you are asked to tune in with your vibrational energetic emotional landscape. This means to expand your awareness of how you feel 100 percent of the time. When you shed tears, it means you are ready to disarm, to drop the sword, to end the fight, and drop the armour around your heart. Give yourself the powerful gift of an emotional release through the shedding of tears. Your inner strength is on the other side of your emotional vulnerability.

Emotional Integrity brings emotional maturity. Emotional maturity brings the realization that, deep down, our sadness is a reflection of how much we have lost touch with our connection to the Universe. We have turned our focus onto others and created judgments about their flaws or faults instead of focusing on what truly matters. Your tears are designed to help you remember the truth—*to love yourself and reclaim your authentic power.*

If you want to experience more love or more meaningful relationships in all areas of your life, then it is time for you to become accountable for how you *feel* and seek a healthier expression in releasing your emotions.

Today's Higher Idea: Check out the Emotional Integrity Process in the Resource section.

Chapter Three
Peace of Mind

As much as transforming your emotions is key to living a happier life, it is also important to know that your mind plays a big role in your quest for happiness and freedom. To become the best or highest version of yourself, your mind must be at peace with itself. This is the journey beyond the familiar.

Peace of mind is a gift you give yourself. To have your thoughts transform from a chaotic state to calmness is a discipline anyone can learn. It is in the stillness of your mind that all duality—positive and negative, good and bad, right and wrong—dissolve.

The reason for all external conflict is simply a reflection of the internal conflict between the many internal selves, your Fallen Angels, and your Soul.

Your Fallen Angels, the invisible dimensions of you, seek your acknowledgment, love, and understanding. As long as they remain unwanted, their voices (your negative thoughts and beliefs) will continually sabotage your happiness. They will not give you the peace of mind you seek. Only when you acknowledge their existence, forgive, love, and integrate their energy into the light of awareness, will your mind begin to calm. If you crave peace in your life, start today connecting your Fallen Angels (below the line) with your Forgotten Angels (above the line). Remember, angels are *angles of light* within. Since *light* is information, looking at situations from a different angle will immediately shift your reality. As you fill your mind, body, and soul with more light you open up to the peace that has always been with you.

Higher Idea #26 Dive into Your Mind

Many years ago, I had a friend and mentor named Steven. He was a very wise man and shared with me the importance of knowing my mind. When explaining the mind, he often referred to Sigmund Freud's theory of personality using the iceberg analogy. He would ask me to use my imagination and see my mind as if it were an iceberg floating in an ocean. Now I ask you to do the same.

The part of the iceberg that is visible above the waterline is the smallest part of the iceberg. Your conscious mind represents the smallest part of the iceberg. Your conscious mind represents the level of awareness you have of your present reality. Your conscious mind can only think one thought at a time. Below the water line the iceberg is vast, and the same is true of your subconscious mind. Your subconscious mind is mostly unknown, until you dive deep and explore its depths.

Your subconscious mind has many layers and is capable of storing every thought, wish, desire, habit, attitude, feeling, and memory from this life—past, parallel, and beyond. Your subconscious mind also controls the natural functions of your body such as circulation, respiration, and digestion. Just as your body functions are on automatic pilot, so too are your behaviour patterns.

The third aspect of your mind, I call your *Divine Mind*, which is like an ocean of flowing intelligence. Your Divine Mind is the gateway to Universal Consciousness or the Source of All That Is, which is experienced in deep trance or meditation. This is where you connect to the genius or Brilliant Self that lives within you.

Your experience in the physical world is played out through these three phases, and within each phase are many layers of complexity. To understand your mind fully, it may take many lifetimes. For now, you are on an evolutionary journey from living with a fear-based mind to spiralling up and embodying your Divine Mind, which plays a big role in living a heart-centered life.

Today's Higher Idea: Talk to a friend about what you are learning.

Higher Idea #27 Put Your Ego in its Place

Your *ego* handles life's issues in three ways; *fight, flee,* or *freeze.* Anytime you choose any of these three ways of reacting, you are living in the Fear Frequency. Your subconscious mind will brand every experience as a negative one if your Fallen Angels (your ego) are in control. Your ego is not a monster. It is more like a frightened child who has been given way too much responsibility.

As I mentioned earlier, your subconscious mind is where all your unacceptable, hidden, or fragmented *selves* exist (your inner Fallen Angels). The *ego* and your many Fallen Angels are synonymous. Unfortunately, if you operate your whole life from the ego perspective, you will experience pain and suffering. The ego's purpose is to keep you living in your small comfort zone as it believes you need to be protected from everything outside your comfort zone. Your *ego* believes life is dangerous, so it will do whatever it takes to keep you separated from the truth. Now, you may want to destroy or get rid of your *ego*; however, I would suggest a higher idea—to put it back in its place of *processing information only* and to stop it from controlling your life.

Every time you say to yourself, "I am fat," "I am stupid," or "I am a loser," you are feeding your ego. Your subconscious mind takes everything you say as truth and goes about creating the reality around you to support your beliefs. This is why it is so important to dismantle any and all negative beliefs you have about yourself and your life. You are a Divine Being of the Universe and there is no one like you.

Transformation begins with self-awareness about who you are. You have the power to change your mind at any time about anything with ease and grace. You have control of the thoughts you think, and when you discover this truth, you raise your vibration.

To take control of your fear-based mind, your *ego*, you are required to reprogram it just as you would a computer. Reprogramming requires influencing your subconscious mind at a cellular or vibrational level, so new empowering truths can be imprinted.

To reprogram a negative state of mind into a higher state of mind is to embrace your spirituality, the higher aspects of who you are. Remember that you are a brilliant being, you are the creator of your life, and you can be, do, and have whatever you wish. Your subconscious mind was designed to be of service to you, not the other way around.

In order to be *joyful* with yourself and your life, it is essential that you create happiness within your mind first. Happiness is realized when you give your life meaning and contribute your positive energy to the world.

A powerful way to direct your *ego* is to invite the higher energies of your Divine Mind into your heart, which will activate your heart's intelligence. Then visualize the higher frequencies of light and color entering into every cell of your body to reactivate your soul's blueprint. The *Divine Mind Conversation* will remind you to speak to your subconscious mind with assertiveness, clarity, absolute love, and respect. Your subconscious mind is here to serve you and as you make the unknown aspects of yourself *known,* you empower yourself.

Another powerful way of directing your mind to a higher vibration, creating more happiness in your life is to release all words from your vocabulary that carry a negative vibration and replace them with higher vibrational words or statements. (I discuss this more in Chapter 5.)

In your past or present relationships can you think back to a disagreement you had and see where your frustration or anger compounded, turning the smallest issue into a mountain of blame. It is because the *ego* will show you images of all the similar scenarios of the past, or all the wrong actions this other man or woman has taken, instead of just focusing on today's issue. Your *ego* loses control the more you stay in the present moment, surrender to *what is,* and focus on what you need to learn about yourself. In fact, letting go of the idea that you *need to be right* will put your ego in its rightful place, which is <u>to process information only</u>. Now you have the power to shift your mind to a higher state of awareness.

Today's Higher Idea: With a trusted friend, talk about what you are learning about yourself and how you have allowed your *ego* to control your life.

Higher Idea #28 Create an Empowered Life Story

Have you defined which Fallen Angels live inside of you and the stories they bring into your life? In Chapter Two, we explored the concept that your Fallen Angels are fragmented *selves* that represent a collective of suppressed intelligent energy. These unwanted *selves* do not want to be trapped in your physical body, and they may be the reason why you act and behave inappropriately at times. All of these inner selves represent soul fragments, and each one carries a story. A story of "I am not good enough," or "I am not worthy," or "I was abused and now I am unlovable," or "I always fail so what is the use?" and so on. Remember, this is not *your* mind. It is mind of the collective—everyone on earth who is living below the line and being controlled by their fear=based thoughts.

Our mind can become divided or fragmented when we have experienced emotional trauma or suffering. We can portray our external self as being strong, powerful, and self-confident in a business meeting or in front of our family and friends, when actually, deep inside, there is that little girl or boy who is feeling alone, afraid, and unloved.

Exploring the many *selves* (fallen and forgotten) and acknowledging their existence will offer you the profound gifts of inner wisdom and insight (*inner sight*) you may have been seeking. Now you have an opportunity to acknowledge the "poor me" story you may have been living out and create a new empowered story.

Peace of mind comes when you have released the chaotic, incorrect thinking that is attached to your old stories. Stories of blame, shame, and guilt will keep you vibrating in the lower realm of fear-based living. Stories of how life is so unfair, hard, difficult, ugly, and miserable will keep you in the muck and chained to a reality created by limiting or false beliefs.

Right now, in this very moment, you have the power to focus on a new, empowered story. A story where all you see is the power you have in creating a beautiful life because you now have a beautiful mind. A story where all you see is beautiful souls who have fallen into a pit of darkness only to open up to the truth of who they are.

Your imagination is the key to creating a new story that empowers us all. As you develop your courage and take the journey beyond the familiar and explore the deepest parts of your mind, body, and soul, you begin to expand your sphere of what is possible for you and for all of us.

Your Fallen Angels also live in your physical body and create the stories of physical pain and suffering. If your body is filled with fear, it will not be able to heal itself. When you release a Fallen Angel you not only liberate your mind you also liberate your body and the limited story that your *dis-ease* is who you are.

When you're in unknown territory, such as exploring your mind, it's always a good idea to have a guide with you, someone you can trust. Your Brilliant Self is always up for a great adventure and is the best of all possible companions. It is your Divine Mind that will introduce you to your Joyful Self, your Creative Self, your Prosperous Self, and your Purposeful Self. As you intentionally connect, embrace, and eventually integrate with these higher levels of consciousness your life will begin to take on a whole new meaning.

So how do you know when you have let go of the wounded stories of your past? When you no longer talk about past events or others in a negative way. When you focus on what is happening right here, right now. When you choose to talk about the vision you have in creating a harmonious world. This will definitely raise your vibration and level of consciousness.

You can make a quantum leap and spiral up into the *Freedom Frequency* when you make the choice to acknowledge, listen, appreciate, and love all your Fallen and Forgotten Angels that live inside of you. Your Fallen Angels will tell you all the false stories you have held on to as truth and your Forgotten Angels will remind you of the empowered story that lives in your heart. They have a great deal to teach you.

Today's Higher Idea: Identify your "poor me" stories of unworthiness, lack, and self-rejection. You are being called to close the old book of your life and open a new book and write out your new, empowered story.

Higher Idea #29 Dismantle Your Limited Beliefs

Have you ever had to pack up all your belongings and move to another city or even across the country? Even if you were moving just across town, you would most likely have many boxes filled with your most valuable possessions. Sometimes we move several times during our lives. It's a lot of work, requiring a lot of time and the organizational skills needed for all the unpacking and clearing out of all the boxes.

How would you feel if you never unpacked or removed those boxes? What if you just lived with those boxes cluttering your space for the rest of your life, not knowing what was in them?

This is what you do with your beliefs. Throughout your life, you have created beliefs (decisions you made about who you are and the reality you live in), placed these beliefs in boxes in your mind, and then forgotten about them. Beliefs can become like cluttered cardboard boxes, filling the mansion of your mind.

Your belief system is programmed from:

- What you have been told to believe from your mother or father, teachers, friends, and/or the media.
- Observations you deem as truth.
- What you tell yourself every moment.

The reality you experience is kept in place by a belief structure. Beliefs are not necessarily true. For example, we once believed we went to the moon only to discover it was a Hollywood stage. We once believed it was impossible that televisions or computers would be in every home. Your belief system can create illusions or truth, lack or abundance, they can create resistance or expand love. Your belief system is either working *against* you or *for* you.

In order for your belief system to work *for* you and create the life you want, you need to become aware of the limited beliefs still stored in your belief mansion. With every piece you don't let go of, you hold yourself back from becoming the woman/man you want to be. The mind becomes filled with out-dated ideas and dysfunctional decisions that leave no room for a new expanded sense of Self. Change in your outer life begins when you transform your mind (your inner *selves*) and integrate them with Source energy, with your Divine Mind.

Expanding your awareness of what you believe, how you think, what you say, and how you act, is key to changing limiting behaviour patterns. It's time to believe and connect with your Forgotten Angels, your inner wisdom. They hold the key to solving all your problems.

Self-esteem grows the more you connect to empowering beliefs about yourself. You came into this world with divine gifts and talents and there is no one like YOU! It takes courage to break through the wall of fear that separates you from these inner gifts. As you cultivate and nurture these higher qualities within you, you will ignite your purpose.

Once you set your mind on where you want to go, life will give you many opportunities to practice, practice, practice. My dad would always say to me, "I believe in you, Karen, and more importantly, I want you to believe in yourself. No matter what challenges life brings, never give up!"

Years ago, I was watching a *Loving Relationship* video by Dr. Gary Smalley. As I was watching him and the impact he had on his audience, I knew I wanted to become a speaker. Yet at that time, I was deathly afraid of speaking in public as I had a limited belief that I would never be good enough or smart enough. The first time I went to a Toastmasters group and had to introduce myself, I could barely get the words out. It took a lot of time and inner work in clearing out my negative beliefs, but it was worth it. Today, I speak in front of large audiences and instead of fear holding me back, I feel a thrill in being of service and sharing my passion. My point is, even though you may not be aware of your purpose, your greatest talent may be hiding behind your greatest fear.

Today's Higher Idea: What do you believe in? What beliefs do you have about yourself and your ability to raise your vibration and live a heart-centered life?

Higher Idea #30 Face Your Fear

Do you know you have secret fears that can hold you back from living your life fully? We all do, until we embrace the courage to consciously explore our own mind from a higher point of view. Acknowledging your fear is one of the first steps in releasing the chains that may bind you. Before a list of fears can be presented, let's first define *fear*. Fear is defined as *the anticipation of pain*. Zig Ziglar claimed that F.E.A.R. has two meanings—*Forget Everything and Run* or *Face Everything and Rise*. The choice is yours!

At the core of the Fear Frequency is your *ego* and your *ego* is in control of all your Fallen Angels. Your *ego* does not want you to discover these aspects of yourself. Why? Because it will lose control and you will become empowered. Your *ego* wants you to stay in the vibration of self-denial, self-rejection, self-doubt, and self-hatred. It does not want you to look within because then you will discover who you are beyond the *self*.

Fear has become a powerful energy force on our planet because of the accumulation of fear-based thinking within the collective consciousness that has had thousands of years to gain power. Fear in itself is *an illusion of your mind*. When you are in fear, you allow your imagination to work *against* you instead of *for* you. The key is remembering that you are not your fear. Instead, begin to see it as energy that moves through you. Fear, in itself, is not a bad thing because it allows you to be cautious and proceed slowly so you can understand your experiences. When you choose to live in the present moment and express love, then you no longer need the energy of fear to be your teacher. This is not about you becoming fearless; this is about you becoming deliciously free.

There are a range of secret fears we have suppressed within our subconscious mind, such as the fear of rejection, fear of loneliness, fear of embarrassment, fear of lack, fear of judgment, fear of losing control, fear of being left behind, fear of being found out, fear of betrayal, fear of pain, fear of loss, fear of what others think, fear of letting go, fear of abandonment, fear of intimacy, fear of not being loved, fear of being wrong, fear of being persecuted for your beliefs, fear of conflict, and fear of your Light. There are many more fears to add to the list; however, this is a good place to start.

Today's Higher Idea: Identify the fear you're ready to face and just sit with it. Feel it. Know it is *not* who you are. It is just energy. Write what thoughts are attached to this fear. To rise up above fear you need to feel safe in your body. What are two things you can do to feel safe? Keep writing! A couple of affirmation to state out loud - "The world is a safe and kind place. I am surrounded by the loving energy of life. I trust myself and the guidance from the universe."

Higher Idea #31 Self-Discipline is About Learning

Many of us cringe upon hearing the word *discipline*. It just sounds so rigid and definitely not fun. Did you know that *discipline* and *disciple* are based on the same root word, which means *to learn?* Self-discipline is about inner motivation and not about controlling others or a means of punishment. Self-discipline is the *focused attention* needed to change your life for the better. You can read about great ideas and strategies that may benefit you, but it takes effort, trust, and courage to act and integrate these principles on a daily basis.

Self-discipline can be seen as a process of devotion to improving all areas of your life and honouring the totality of who you are mentally, spiritually, emotionally, and physically. If your thoughts are scattered, if you are easily triggered to anger, or procrastinate on projects, then discipline of thought, behaviour, and action will be required to follow through with decisions that can better your life. Choose to see self-discipline as the path that leads you to greater pleasures in life.

Discipline is making the choice between what you want now and what you want the most.

- Author unknown

For example, self-discipline is when a man/woman who wants a relationship to last, will do everything to stop the sabotaging beliefs and destructive behaviours that are destroying it.

When you take control of your mental dimension and put your mind in order, you will experience less chaos. Everything in the Universe works together. By educating yourself, you'll learn that the primary law of creation is *order*. Even though life may appear to be chaotic at the core, there is order—*a reason for everything we experience.* Even traffic jams appear to be chaotic, but every driver has a destination.

Today's Higher Idea: View self-discipline as self-love or self-devotion to a higher way of living.

Higher Idea #32 Breathe in the Energy of Patience

Have you ever had a mental meltdown? Have you been confused as to why things are not happening the way you want them to? Have you stomped around yelling at the Universe, *"What's going on now? I shouldn't have to do this. This shouldn't be happening to me. I am a good man/woman. I want my beautiful life NOW"!* I have said these exact words many times. I believe we all have moments of ranting and raving when a dream is not being realized or we just don't seem to be manifesting what we want.

Freedom is a choice, and becoming free requires patience. Patience is not about waiting. Patience is required to move from the world you live in now to the world you want to create. Patience is the gap between the current *you* and the Brilliant YOU *(the butterfly analogy I mention in the introduction)* that is waiting to emerge. Patience is the space required for deep reflection as you take the journey in remembering your Divine nature.

Young ones and seniors can be fabulous teachers of patience because they show you how to be in the moment. You will know you have cultivated patience when you no longer experience road rage. Everyone is showing you the path to staying in the present moment, which is where your power lies. Whether you are waiting for others or waiting for a dream to be realized, it is in those moments of waiting that you are being called to reflect on any incompletions or unresolved issues that need to be addressed or acted upon.

The practice of daily meditation and deep breathing will also empower you in fully embracing the energy of patience. In patience, we allow the many invisible selves to blossom and transform. When you are patient with yourself, you will then experience patience with others.

I also recommend you practice the *Divine Mind Conversation* (Higher Idea #79) to help you remember your Patient Self.

Today's Higher Idea: Whenever you feel you do not have the willingness or tolerance for delay, see this as an opportunity for deep reflection on present issues in your life. Smile! Tell yourself that you are choosing to be patient as this is how you want others to be with you.

Higher Idea #33 Breathe in the Energy of Trust

In order for you to experience integration with any of your Forgotten Angels that live above the line, you will first need to breathe in the energy of trust. The energy of trust carries a firm belief in who you are as a Divine being. Trust in yourself. Trust in others. Trust in the universe.

Trust transforms belief into knowing and then knowing into remembering. Trust is having the knowledge that you possess the inner strength and ability to move through every situation or opportunity that life offers you. Trust is having the knowledge that whatever you attract in your life is guiding you to a higher learning. The world of trust is very powerful, and your Trusting Self will take you on a most incredible journey to deeper worlds beyond the physical dimension.

As you remember the power of trust and breathe it into your heart center, you will trust yourself and the world around you. In order to experience trust in others, trust must blossom within you. As you deepen into your spiritual journey and breathe in trust, you will remember that the universe is safe and supportive.

The more you align and create a relationship with your Forgotten Angels, the more you'll trust the inner voice of wisdom, the voice of Intuition. Trust that no matter what happens, you are meant to experience it for the evolution of Self. A woman/man who trusts herself/himself can quickly make a decision, get off the fence, and move forward knowing that whichever direction she or he has chosen will be a great adventure.

Today's Higher Idea: Trust that you are always safe, and that the universe supports and loves you.

Higher Idea #34 Remember Your Divine Mind

Your Divine Mind is the cosmic upper realm that envelops both the conscious and subconscious minds. Your Divine Mind is your heart's intelligence and is in every atom of your being. It is where your inner Forgotten Angels (your authentic aspects of self) resonate and where your connection to All That Is takes place.

Remember, your subconscious mind and conscious mind must be in alignment in order for you to transform your life. Your subconscious transforms more rapidly when your Divine Mind is utilized and linked to your emotional dimension. In other words, when you connect your imagination with the power of higher thought vibrations and emotions, you can then explore your subconscious as an empowered being and transform all limitations into freedom.

Your Divine Mind exists in the realm of pure genius; it's all around and within you. It's quite literally *everywhere* and the core essence of your Divine Mind is enlightened love and harmony. This realm carries the information of your soul's purpose and the blueprint of your Brilliant Self, the highest version of you. This is where all insights, ideas, and creative sparks of genius exist, all waiting for you to consciously align your vibration to this realm of Divinity and access Source energy.

You are either operating from your fear-based mind, which keeps you in limitation or you are operating from your Divine Mind, which is the journey beyond the familiar. Your Divine Mind will always take you outside of your comfort zone and beyond the radar screen of your mind, as this is where all manifested dreams reside.

Harmony of mind occurs when you explore the unknown subconscious mind and Divine Mind and bring them into your conscious awareness. It is here that you develop intimacy (into-me-I-see) with your inner Fallen Angels (distorted intelligence) and your Forgotten Angels (hidden intelligence), which transforms you into the Remembered Angel (higher intelligence).

Today's Higher Idea: State out loud, "With divine intention I now ask my Brilliant Self to show me the way so I can release all fear and negative energies from my mind consciousness system with ease and grace. I ask my Higher Self to download the information I require to move forward in the direction of my heart desires. And so it is."

Now let go and trust that you will receive the guidance you are seeking.

Chapter Four
Open Your Brilliant Heart

Have you lived your life with a guarded heart or an open heart? If you have closed your heart due to the fear of being hurt, then an energetic heart wall is created. This wall will definitely keep out the hurt and pain, but it will also keep out the love, joy, and prosperity you may be seeking.

A heart that is guarded or closed is unable to fulfill the dream it is here to realize. It will also hold you back from connecting to all your Forgotten Angels (positive qualities) that vibrate in the higher realms such as your Joyful Self, your Loving Self, your Sensual Self, your Passionate Self, and so on. The loneliness and unnecessary suffering you experience is caused from the separation from Source, what I have termed *spiritual vacancy*. This absence of love for yourself (*selves*) is the root of so much pain and suffering.

The walls around your heart are created by your Fallen Angels, the voices within that say, "Do not trust men/women" or "Love means getting hurt" or "Love is painful." If you believe this, you have been deceived into believing a lie. This invisible demonic realm feeds off your fearful emotions, and as long as you remain in the *fear frequency* you will experience manipulation, betrayal, neglect, and so on. When you are in the Freedom Frequency of life, you will only attract those who are respectful and honest, who deeply care and wish only the best for you.

Your heart is very intelligent. New research from The Institute of HeartMath (see Resources section) states that the heart is the most powerful generator of electromagnetic energy in our bodies, producing the largest rhythmic electromagnetic field of any of the body's organs. The heart's electrical field is about sixty times greater in amplitude than the electrical activity generated by the brain. The magnetic field produced by the heart is more than 5,000 times greater in strength than the field generated by the brain, and it can be detected a number of feet away from the body.

You are being called to expand your capacity to receive and give more love. If you have ever experienced heartache, it is because your heart is actually expanding, breaking open to truth, and deepening into s*elf-love*.

When you become consciously aware of the power you possess in your heart, all your challenges, issues, and shortcomings will dissolve. Your heart has the intelligence to bring forth all you desire with ease and grace. When your heart and mind are aligned, you are divinely powerful. With the practice of meditation, breath work, visualization, and devotion, you have the power to release all perceived negative forces from your heart center so you can live a heart-centered life. When your heart is fully open to the nurturing qualities of giving and receiving *love,* you are *free.* The effort is worth it.

Living a heart-centered life begins by embracing self-love, then relationship love, then community love, and then we expand to worldly love and unite in enlightened love.

Higher Idea #35 Live in Enlightened Love

As I mentioned in Chapter One, the core essence of the *Freedom Frequency* is *love.* This love does not compare to physical love, romantic love, sexual love, or friendship love. This is the realm of *Enlightened Love,* and it is the highest vibration we can experience as Divine beings.

Enlightened love is like having heaven open up inside of you and all pain (mental, emotional, spiritual, and physical) vanishes completely, leaving you in a state that is beyond bliss and beyond any physical happiness you may have experienced.

Enlightened love is the glue that binds everything. It is an expanded awareness or state of being where you see the personality of others, and yet at the same time, you acknowledge the divinity (the soul) within every woman/man.

You will know you are resonating in the vibration of enlightened love when you meet someone and all you see is another version of yourself standing before you. Now you have remembered that you are *one* with all of life.

You may have experienced a taste of this higher love on occasion when you have had a direct spiritual experience in meditation or in sharing an extraordinary experience with others. To fully live in this higher vibration of love, it is critical to take the journey in disciplining the ego, the Fallen Angels within. Compassionate discipline stirred with the devotion of spiritual fulfillment is a path anyone can take toward embracing the higher vibrations of enlightened love.

As much as you crave love, you may find yourself hiding from it. Deep down, there may be an intense *fear* of love. Why? Because the *ego* does not want you to remember your own Divine nature. It will create an energetic wall of resistance every time you step into the light of higher love.

Enlightened love is a high intensity vibration and so far, only a small percentage of beings on the planet are able to sustain this level of consciousness, as most of us do not know how to embody it. The vibration can feel uncomfortable because you are not used to feeling this powerful force move through your body. If you have been hiding for a long period of time in the darkness of the fear frequency, you can become very afraid of the unknown, of who you are, of where you are going, of connecting with others, or of being vulnerable. When the truth is, the only thing you are here on this planet for, is *love*, to be *love*, to remember you are LOVE, and then take inspired action and treat others as you would like to be treated.

In my course, The Evolution of Relationships, *enlightened love* is the fifth cycle you experience once you have spiralled up through the four cycles of integration. Enlightened love is living in alignment with Source energy and recognizing that all relationships are designed to empower, uplift, and encourage. The main purpose of any relationship in today's world, which includes the relationships you have with your mother/father, sons/daughters, siblings, friends, coworkers, partner or spouse, is to empower you in becoming the best version of yourself.

To connect to the vibration of enlightened love you are called to learn all you can about how to dissolve the heart-wall (Higher Idea #41) that has kept you closed off from fully loving yourself and others. You must release the bonds of yesterday and renew your own heart's intelligence. How can you say you are in love with someone if you have yet to explore your own heart?

The purpose of any relationship is to serve each other's growth and spiritual emergence. You attract others into your life for your own expansion; spiritually, mentally, emotionally, and physically. When you are in any relationship and you uplift instead of squashing the spirit, there is profound growth that occurs. Enlightened love relationships are experienced as a deep soul love for another and for life.

Many of us are afraid of losing our identity in intimate relationships. The amazing thing is that you are *meant* to lose your identity, the identity of your *ego,* so you realign with your true identity as a Divine Being who is a powerful and heart-centered creator.

Every relationship you have with others reflects the relationship you have with yourself. If your relationship squashes your spirit in the form of constant arguing, blame, and criticism, it is time to take your power back. If you are squashing the spirit of others, then it is time to restore self-love. If you have the willingness to learn new and healthier ways of relating, you can re-ignite the spirit of empowerment in any relationship. The more you spiral up out of the fear frequency, the more your physical body becomes less dense, allowing the higher selves, your Forgotten Angels, to fill your body with the energies of *enlightened love*. You have the capacity to embody these eternal forces in your life by opening up your heart and remembering the brilliance that is you.

True freedom of being comes from diving deep into your subconscious mind, shifting perceptions of who you are, and spiralling up through your energy centers into your heart.

Today's Higher Idea: Your heart is wise; listen to it. When you make the choice to live from your heart, you will be empowered with a divine force of higher intelligence.

Higher Idea #36 Forgive Yourself

As I journeyed beyond the familiar and descended further down the stairs of my subconscious mind, I realized that my past would always haunt me until I had forgiven others and especially myself for all my perceived wrongdoings, lies, and destructive behaviours. The path to forgiveness was not easy, but I knew that in order for me to spiral up out of the fear frequency and into the Freedom Frequency, I needed to embody the energy of forgiveness. I struggled with forgiveness most of my life. I felt if I forgave the men who had raped me, I was making what they did to me okay. The hate I carried in my heart toward men consumed me. As much as I hated men, I desperately wanted to be in a relationship with a loving man. As my spirituality deepened, I realized that if I were to attract respectful and loving men into my life, I would first need to forgive the Masculine self within. I would also need to forgive and release the negative stories and beliefs I had wrapped around men.

Forgiving the men of my past included my ex-husband, cheating or abusive boyfriends, my father, my brother, and *all men* throughout time for their perceived wrongdoings of destruction, violence, abuse, neglect, and rape toward the feminine. This profound level of forgiveness was one of the biggest gifts I could ever have given myself.

What I found more difficult was forgiving myself, which meant the acknowledgment of all *my* perceived wrongdoings, dark secrets, and the harm I may have caused others, whether it was emotional, spiritual, or physical. The Emotional Integrity Process (see Resources section) allowed me to get real with the emotions and mental images I had suppressed in the many vaults of my memory banks. I sobbed uncontrollably as my life movie played before my mind's eye. I knew that the hundreds of images flashing before me were releasing all the negatively charged energy I had concealed. I even had surprising images surface as I saw my Inner Rapist, who showed me how I had raped women in a previous life. My Mean self, my Critical self, and my Hateful self showed up as the mirrors of self-reflection. I heard the words, *"Everything I have done unto others, I will eventually experience myself."* I saw the karmic effects of all my actions and how every individual was playing his or her role so perfectly to reflect back how I saw myself. As the emotional pain subsided, I knew my Forgiving Self had found her way to me. I actually felt my energetic heart opening as I crossed the bridge of forgiveness into enlightened love. My intention was to live in this state of bliss forever.

The energy of forgiveness opened me up and connected me to my Peaceful Self, my Respectful Self, my Compassionate Self, and my Loving Self. These *Selves*, who I had actually forgotten, showed me how to see my body differently, to love my body, and therefore, to respect and value myself wholly and completely.

The Unforgiving self lives below the line, refuses to forgive, and makes no allowance for error. The Unforgiving self carries the seed of all things *unforgiving*, and as long as this self remains in control, the heart will remain closed. To create a beautiful life, you will need to connect to your Forgiving Self. Your Forgiving Self has the power to unlock the heavy chains that bind you to the fear frequency.

Self-love is the bridge from living in fear to crossing over and living in the Freedom Frequency of life. Self-love is realized through self-forgiveness. Learning to forgive the many Fallen Angels that live inside of you and forgiving yourself for ignoring or rejecting these aspects of yourself, will open you up to the energy of *deserve-ability* and to cross the bridge into the Freedom Frequency of life. Once you are above the line, there is nothing to forgive, as you are living in the love vibration.

Our past is just a memory, and memories are made up of moments. It is a moment in time that creates an experience, and then we judge that experience as either good/bad or right/wrong. If we deem the experience wrong, then our Protector self will show up and believe it needs to guard our heart. Our Protector self will then constantly remind us of this past moment in time by taking the same feeling about that one moment and making it our whole life story— when in reality, it was only a moment in time.

It is your Forgiving Self that will help you view your past from a higher perspective so you can recreate a new empowered memory of every moment. Everyone in your life who you believe has caused you grief, pain, or suffering has come into your life to remind you to stop playing small, to stand up for yourself, and to live boldly in the direction of your dreams. Forgiveness blossoms when you know everyone is reflecting aspects of yourself that you have yet to embrace.

Sometimes it's difficult to forgive, especially if you have lost your job, your home, or a loved one. Once you embrace the world of forgiveness, you realize that it's a powerful means of cutting negative energy cords from others in your life. The more you forgive yourself and your own perceived negative behaviours and actions, the more you forgive the negative behaviours and actions (Fallen Angels) in others.

When you are living above the line, the energy of forgiveness is no longer necessary. There is nothing to forgive when you are vibrating in the *Freedom Frequency* of life, for here you are the embodiment of Compassion. It is here you recognize the divinity in yourself and the divinity in others. You recognize that everyone is fully accountable for every experience, thought, and feeling they have. You will only attract others who vibrate in the same frequency of thoughtfulness and compassion. Tragedy, drama, and trauma live below the line.

Today's Higher Idea: Become present to who you are *being*. Look in the mirror and make direct eye contact with yourself. Look deep into your eyes and say, *"I love you. I'm sorry. Please forgive me. I appreciate you."*

Higher Idea #37 You Are a Valuable Divine Being

See yourself as a valuable Divine being. Self worth is increased when you connect to your *Worthy Self.* Your *Worthy Self* lives by a value system that is defined by you and not by the opinions of others. Your values are defined by what's important to you; for example, health, living authentically, freedom, service to others, creativity, love, and truth. Once you have established your core values—what is important to you—you can use them as a filter in making any important decision. Your values will help you filter others, business opportunities, or events. If you feel there is an alignment with your values, then proceed. If not, you know to move on.

Your values determine what kind of man/woman you are. An important fact to remember is that your own sense of value is determined by what you believe about yourself and not by what you have. Remember, your goals and intentions need to be in alignment with your values; otherwise, you may need to change direction. A simple reality check to figure out where you're at in any given moment is to ask yourself, "Am I in alignment with my deepest core values?"

Only you can determine your own set of values and once you do, trust that they will always guide you in the right direction. When you integrate your values, you will make better and healthier choices based on your sense of self-worth. You will naturally lift your life up and attract others who resonate with the same values as you.

Remember, there is nothing more valuable in this world than YOU! You are a Divine Being of infinite power and potential.

Today's Higher Idea: Visit my website (see Resources section) to view a list of values. Write down five core values with which you feel you are in alignment. Use the *Divine Mind Conversation* method to connect to your Valuable Self and see what message is awaiting you.

Higher Idea #38 Nurture Your Soul

How often do you connect to your soul? Do you know it exists? How did you nurture your soul this week? There are many of us who have no idea that our souls even exist. We all have a loving soul, born ready to embrace our earthly purpose. Yet if our egos, our Fallen Angels, are allowed to rule, the soul is locked away, undernourished, and forgotten. The ego is determined to squash trust, imagination, and creativity, and it views vulnerability as a weakness. We may even build energetic walls around our heart in order to protect what we believe about ourselves.

Many of us relate only to our own physical needs, wants, and desires, living with little or no regard for others. Those of us who live that way have yet to connect with our heart and soul. This is not wrong, as every soul is being revived in divine time.

Right now, consciousness is evolving and men and women are becoming mindful of and discovering a deeper sense of purpose. We have begun exploring the spiritual realms and deeper truths of our souls. By exploring the spiritual dimension, you discover the truth about who you are and the purpose of your existence. During this journey to the heart, many life lessons are learned and are essential if a higher love is to be realized.

Living above the line requires nurturing of the soul. If your soul is under-nurtured then your freedom of choice is limited. You always have the power to make necessary daily choices, but if you are making your decisions from a place of fear (ego), you may remain a victim of circumstance in which your only focus is survival and experiencing an unfulfilled life.

The day I woke up spiritually, I could not stop the tears from flowing. I had read books about the soul, but now I was experiencing a profound part of me I never really knew existed before. I could not stop apologizing to my soul for ignoring it for so many years. My *soul* was like a long[lost friend who knew everything about me and loved me unconditionally.

Today's Higher Idea: Place your attention on your heart and visualize a flame in the center. This flame symbolizes the *light of your soul*. It's up to you to ignite the light within and expand your soul power.

Higher Idea #39 Connect to Your Inner Young Self

Laughter, play, joy, fun, innocence, and *being in the moment* are a few qualities your Inner Young Self can bring into your life. If you are not connected to this very real part of you, your life can be constantly influenced by an emotionally wounded Young Self within who inhabits an adult body. We all have an inner Young Self (Little Girl or Little Boy), the aspect of us that holds the sum of all our childhood memories, and the more we tune into this aspect of ourselves the more we open the door to profound healing.

I believe there is a defining moment when a youth experiences trauma and is not able to cope with the destructive energies in their environment, and therefore, in protecting itself, the mind becomes fragmented, separating itself from reality. Our Young Self then hides deep down inside of us only to be possessed by the Protector self. This Fallen Angel may whisper, "Let me out and I will make you strong. You will never have to experience this sadness or loneliness again." Convinced that this inner voice is true, the frightened Young Self says, "Yes," and the light of our innocence becomes buried. From this point forward, we grow up and live our life believing we are strong when in fact we're experiencing life through our Forgotten Young Self who throws temper tantrums and bullies his/her way through life.

We unconsciously and unknowingly lock away our Young Self as we take on the role of being a mature man or woman and all the responsibilities, stresses, and expectations that go along with it. We become robots on automatic pilot. Meanwhile, our soul waits patiently for us to wake up to the innocent Young Self within and remember the joy that lives in our heart.

This experience is a natural part of your earthly journey and, at some point in your life, you will be called to go within and reunite with your Young Self. Relationship breakdown due to a lack of intimacy is the end result of a neglected and unloved Young Self. The Divine Mind Conversation will teach you how to nurture and guide your Young Self with the love and the nurturing it needs so you can fully release the emotional chains of your past and spiral up above the line.

Today's Higher Idea: Your Young Self is here to remind you to have a sense of humour and to stop taking life so seriously. Do whatever it takes to bring more laughter and joy into your life. Allow yourself to feel vulnerable. Go outside and spend a day playing.

Higher Idea #40 Be the Love that You Are

We have programmed ourselves to criticize others instead of uplifting them. We have been programmed to create separation instead of connection. For these destructive patterns to disappear, we are being called to remember our Forgotten Angels. We are being called to remember that love is at the core of who we are, and that we need to do whatever it takes to express love from that part of ourselves.

You may crave love and yearn to be loved, yet if your Fallen Angels are in control, the moment you experience even a glimpse of love, they are programmed to shut you down. Your Fallen Angels will communicate to you through your thoughts, which will affect how you feel, and therefore, affect how you act over the smallest of issues. If you do not know how to control the energy that is moving through you, they will direct you to close up, be afraid to feel, or stop you from receiving and giving love. Your inner Fallen Angel voices may then tell you to run away, to fight, to escape, or to move on. Do not listen! Instead do whatever it takes to break open to love. Drop into vulnerability and talk about your fear, let your tears be released, breathe, and just SIT in the energy that is moving through your body. This energy will pass, and harmony can be restored in moments. It is your choice.

When you transcend the ego or Fearful self, you let go of the idea that you are the center of the universe and everything revolves around you. Once you have released your ego from controlling your life, you are able to drop down from living in your head to living in your heart. This means you can come home from work and actually be fully present and engaged with your beloved and family. When you are being the love that you are, you can make eye contact, listen to what is being said without judgment, and keep your tone of voice to a welcoming level. When you know that you are energetically connected to everyone, you will be less likely to harm another. Higher knowledge is remembering that any inner pain you project outside of yourself is guaranteed to boomerang back, causing your energy vibration to drop.

To live in the Freedom Frequency, you will be required to fully define the man or woman you want to be. Relationships offer the most powerful growth opportunity to deepen into love for yourself and to understand what it means to be *love* in action. Any relationship—whether it is with your father or mother, your beloved, your siblings, or your friends—will offer a time and space for you to discover and express your Loving Self, your Cruel self, your Angry self, your Happy Self, and so on. Everyone you relate to will mirror an aspect of you, showing you what *Selves* still require your attention. Can you be the first one who steps into love? Can you be the first one to apologize, or the first one to give a hug, or the first one to admit you misunderstood?

You can save yourself much grief and experience a drama-free and stress-free life by learning to connect with your heart intelligence. When you are open to learning from others, your heart is open. When you are not open to learning about yourself, you are vibrating at a lower frequency and your heart remains guarded. Remember, love cannot be taken away. Love does not cause pain. Love does not cause the heart to ache. Only the lack of love can cause pain and heartache.

Start today and connect with your Loving Self. Once you have an appreciation for who you are and can see others for who they truly are, you will connect with the vibrations of love, the unified field that links you to the blueprint of your destiny. Now you can focus your attention on creating value in your life and sharing your soul inspired talents with the world. Life will support you in the most incredible and magical ways.

Love is the glue that binds everything together in physical reality. I suggest you put your focus on the vibration of love so you can manifest everything you want.

Today's Higher Idea: What if you discovered that *you* are the love you seek? Close your eyes and breathe the energy of love into your chest. As you exhale, breathe out love energy to all who are open to receiving it. Do this ten times slowly and with intention. Do you feel expansive, unlimited, and connected?

Higher Idea #41 Breaking Down the Heart Wall

With all the tragedy on the planet, we may well wonder, *How can the Universe be a loving place?* Tragedy occurs when we walk through life with a closed or guarded heart. Love is the most powerful force, and if you are not willing to express love, life seems to have a way of orchestrating events that will break our hearts open to *feeling.* Why do we need an illness, an accident, or a death in the family to break down the walls of separation and force everyone together to forgive and open our hearts?

Everyone has an energetic *heart wall,* whether we are aware of it or not. The *heart wall* was created to protect you from hurt and pain when you were young, but now it can be the root cause of what holds you back from achieving your dreams or experiencing a fulfilling relationship.

I became aware of my *heart wall* when I had a direct experience of the Divine twenty years ago. Up to that point, I had no idea that a heart-wall even existed. However, I was shown this energetic wall wrapped tightly around my heart, and this wall was an accumulation of layers upon layers of dark energy (trapped negative emotions). In that moment, I knew that my deepest purpose was to do whatever it took to dissolve these layers so I could experience the power of *enlightened love* in my life.

Today this information about the *heart-wall* has been scientifically proven. Dr. Bradley Nelson, a renowned holistic physician and author of *The Emotion Code*, reveals how emotionally charged events from your past can still be haunting you in the form of "trapped emotions" around your heart.

Love cannot be taught, bought, borrowed, or stolen. Love can only be felt through an open heart. When your heart is open, you resonate with the higher vibrations of love, health, joy, and prosperity. Love is a responsibility that teaches us the *ability to respond* to life instead of reacting. Responsibility is learning to become aware of your inner power and to recognize when you are either exerting your power over others or giving it away. When you allow others to trigger lower energies, such as anger or hate, you are giving up your power. Your power is in being kind, respectful, and keeping your heart open—no matter what.

Your heart closes because you feel separate from others, yourself, or life. Your heart opens when you have loving thoughts about others and especially when you have loving thoughts about yourself. Remembering to reclaim, embrace, and love the many Fallen and Forgotten Angels alive inside of you is a powerful way to dissolve the *heart-wall*. Each Fallen Angel is linked to a perceived negative emotion and the more you allow yourself to feel and release these trapped layers of heavy energy, the more *life-force* energy can fill your heart, dissolving all hurt and pain.

Meditation and deep breathing are a beautiful way to open your heart to yourself. Opening your heart is a choice you can make right now. You can choose to say, "I am remembering to love myself. I now choose to love and appreciate my heart's intelligence. I know I am safe, and I now choose to trust myself. I now choose to live a heart-centered life."

When your brilliant heart is open, your natural gifts and talents unfold and creativity manifests. Allow yourself to become vulnerable. Through this state of openness, your mind and heart become one and you expand to a higher level of consciousness, which will dramatically change your life for the better.

Today's Higher Idea: A beautiful daily practice is to ask your inner guides and teachers of love and light, who vibrate in the spiritual dimension, for assistance. You can say, "By Divine intention, I ask my Higher Self to assist in opening my heart and dissolving my heart-wall with ease and grace. I now choose to let go of my fear of loving others. I now make a conscious choice to be the love I AM. I now choose to love myself and trust life. I now choose to see that the universe supports me. And so it is."

Higher Idea #42 Love Your Body

Have you ever heard someone with low self-esteem say, *"I am just a human being?"* Starting today, I suggest you see yourself as a *Divine being.* Remember, your physical body is the temple that houses your soul. You are here to take care of this Divine temple so you can experience all the richness of life. You are now being asked to release the story of being wounded, damaged, and frail. As long as you keep repeating and believing in these lower ideas, you will remain in a cycle of weakness.

Through alternative medicine, energy work, and infusing my body with the higher vibrations of love in the form of sound, color, and light, I was able to heal my body of chronic back pain, fatigue, IBS, depression, allergies, and transmuted ovarian cancer cells. I believe our bodies are so intelligent that they *know* how to heal themselves.. In fact, the physical body is so intelligent that it can often produce substances similar to the drugs prescribed by a doctor. For example, when your mind is calm and peaceful, your body will produce a state similar to that induced by Valium. The vibrations within the Freedom Frequency will bring forth a profound state of love similar to that created by the drug Ecstasy. We're all capable of producing these natural states that bring forth feelings of incredible peace, comfort, and love, without the disastrous side effects of synthetic or chemically manufactured drugs.

Where love does not exist, illness makes a home. I am not sure where I read these words of deep truth, but these simple words have inspired me to learn how to love my body and to open my heart to who I am as a woman. Through the expansion of self-love, I began to understand and accept the direction in which my life was moving. Hating or disliking any part of my body allowed my body to remain in its ugly state because its ugly state was all I could see. As I began to love every part of my body, my body began to transform into the body I had always dreamed of having—naturally.

The worlds of health, wellness, and longevity are available to you. If these worlds are important to you, then begin at once to let go of the diseased and frail ideas you have about yourself. You need to eliminate words like *illness, weak, frail, wounded, kill,* and *damaged* from your vocabulary and replace them with new, empowering statements such as: "I am feeling incredible strength within my body," or "I now release my wounded stories," or "My body vibrates in total health." You'll be amazed by how your body changes when you focus on the health template that is already imprinted in your cells. Remember, thoughts have the power to create illness or a higher vibration of health in your body. What you focus on expands, so think higher thoughts and you'll experience a journey to new worlds you never knew existed.

Health is your natural state. Connecting to your Healthy Self will bring the energy vibrations of optimal health into every cell of your body. When you feel ill, you're vibrating in the frequency of fear. At that point, it's important to do whatever it takes to change your focus and spiral up in your thoughts, words, and actions. Express loving words such as "I love you body. I am sorry. Please forgive me."

My suggestions are not intended to replace the services and advice of your physician. I am here to share higher knowledge that can completely change your world for the better. We live in a society that spoon-feeds drugs and supplements to us. Doctors who practice Western-style medicine have a great purpose, which is to assist those who live in the Frequency of Fear. Those who vibrate above the line are tuned into the truth that we are already whole and complete and there is nothing to heal. This is a journey, a transformative journey, which many around the world are living today.

All I ask is that you do your research. Question everything. You're much stronger in mind, body, and spirit than you have been led to believe. Your body knows when you do not love it. It's time to recognize that your body is not just material flesh, but energy made up of light vibrations. Light carries information and vibrates at a very high frequency. If your body is full of heavy, fear-based energies, it will block the light or life force energy from rejuvenating the body to an optimal level of health.

I highly recommend an excellent book called *You Can Heal Your Life* by Louise L. Hay. In the book, Hay provides *The List*, an invaluable reference exploring the correlation between a disease and the probable psychological cause.

As a result of the spiritual coaching work I do, I've discovered that many illnesses we experience are rooted in our mental and emotional dimensions. Our thoughts have become weak and dysfunctional. When your mind and body do not relate to one another, it causes inner turmoil. As long as an inner struggle is occurring between your body and mind, you will experience a lack of ease. The cure is to arrange and bring order to an otherwise chaotic state of mind. It is vitally important to make every effort to build a relationship with your body that demands respect. You can no longer take your body for granted. You can let go of the idea that you need to have a man-made body, and step into your power as a Divine being, loving the form that you have been given by our Creator.

Today's Higher Ideas:

Raise your vibration through exercise.

Your body wants to move. Learn to listen to the wisdom of your body. Your body is always speaking to you. The more you move your body, the more energy and mental clarity you have to handle life's challenges. When your legs want to run, they will tell you. When your body wants to stretch, you may be drawn to practice yoga. The key is in following through with your body's request. It knows what it needs. Exercise is an expression of self-love, *body love.*

Raise your vibration by eating high vibrational food.

Women/men who vibrate at a higher frequency only fuel themselves with high vibrational food because they love and respect their bodies. Low vibrational foods, such as meat, processed or fast foods, do not make you feel good after you have eaten it. High vibrational foods such as fruits and vegetables, make you feel light and energized. Your body will never ask for fast or processed food. It is only the *ego mind* that seeks to be filled with toxic energy. Commit today to becoming consciously aware of what you eat and how you feel after you eat. This is an important step in having the energy you need to live your beautiful life. David Wolfe is one of my favourite authors and I love listening to his presentations and videos regarding raw and super foods. (See Resource section)

Raise Your Vibration with Sound Therapy.

Science and western medicine are finally validating what shamans have known for a millennium: that the healing energy of sound vibrations such as tuning fork therapy, listening to Baroque, the playing of crystal bowls, or any sound that harmonizes with the frequency of the heart, will increase the health vibration of your physical body.

You can tap into the power to transform your physical body and align with your optimal health template. After all, health is your natural state of being.

Higher Idea #43 The Power of Your Breath

The most important thing in life is your *breath*. Without breath, you would not exist for more than a few minutes. One of the most powerful tools for opening your heart to love is learning how to breathe deeply. When you deepen your relationship with *breath,* you deepen into love.

Few of us truly understand the importance of deep breathing. Breathing is life itself. When you are consciously breathing you know you are breathing much more than "just air." You are actually breathing in the same Source energy, life-force energy that creates universes. Prana or life-force energy feeds the mind, body, and soul; it is the connection to eternal health. We have become shallow breathers, but it's time to become one with the life-force energy that fills our bodies and breathe deeply into our belly.

Proper breathing from the diaphragm, cycling through the heart and all the energy centers within the body, can increase your capacity to discharge toxic energy. Deep breathing worked miracles for me in helping me to transform my dis-ease into a body that moved through life with ease.

Deep conscious breathing is when you are fully aware of each breath. You feel it. You embrace it. The benefits of deep-belly breathing are:

- Assists in releasing fear energies
- Brings more oxygen into your body

- Deepens your sexual expression
- Improves concentration
- Reduces stress and revitalizes your body
- Brings you into the present moment
- Deepens the communication between mind, body, and soul
- Integrates your spiritual, mental, emotional, and physical selves

Today's Higher Idea: Practice Higher Idea #44 on the next page.

Higher Idea #44 Your Daily Deep Breathing Practice

Following are a few simple things you can do whenever you feel stressed or anxious. Deep-belly breathing will instantly calm your mind and bring the higher vibrations of relaxation.

- Find a private place where you know you will not be disturbed. Outside in nature is perfect.

- Sit in a comfortable chair with your back straight. Close your eyes. Now take a deep, slow, five-second breath in through your nose…take it all the way down into your belly. Then exhale for the same length of time through your nose.

- As soon as you have exhaled, inhale again to the count of five. Keep each breath naturally connected to the one before it. Do not pause between inhalation and exhalation.

- Now that you are comfortable breathing this way, visualize Prana (life-force) as a gold light entering your nostrils with each breath you inhale. Visualize a wave of this coloured light spiralling down into all the parts of your body that feel tight and tense. Keep your focus on your breath as you now intentionally bring this life force energy into your heart center, filling this area with love.

- Next, bring the breath slowly down into your belly and allow this energy to expand into all your organs. Each inhalation and exhalation is a cycle. With each cycle, inhale in the energy of health, then exhale dis-ease; inhale peace, exhale stress; inhale love, exhale fear. With every exhale you are releasing this energy from your body and sending it back to Source. Cycle through ten times or until you feel a shift in your energy.

- Now you're ready to face the world once again.

Deep-belly conscious breathing gives you more energy, greater mental clarity, and a higher level of trust in yourself.

Today's Higher Idea: When you feel stress or frustration building, practice deep-belly breathing.

Higher Idea #45 Breathe in Compassion

The first step in cultivating compassion is to have empathy for others. We all have the power to create heaven on earth when we breathe in the energy of compassion and send it out through our hearts to those who are suffering.

If your aim in life is to be happy, then become compassionate and caring. Many of us lack compassion and empathy for others because our hearts are closed to the giving and receiving of love. If we are self-centered, we only focus on our own needs and ignore the needs of others.

Having sympathy for someone is very different than having compassion. Sympathy means feeling sorry for others, which causes you to become caught in the emotional entangled energies of the one who suffers. You are not here to take on others' energy. You are here to dive into your own Suffering self and as you do, you automatically tap into the vibration of the collective consciousness of all who suffer. As you dissolve the suffering seed within yourself, through the assistance of your own Compassionate Self, you contribute to the evolution of us all. This is how important you are. Remember, we are all energetically connected.

This inner work allows you to tune into how others must feel in times of deep despair, sadness, and loneliness. This understanding will empower you to see the reasons for the behaviour of those who have mistreated you. As you learn to have more compassion for yourself, you will begin to have more compassion for others. Now you can hold space for others, through listening and being present to their needs.

Breathe in the energy of compassion that is already you. Compassion happens when you live with an open heart. When you are open, you have no reason to fear anything. Compassion brings forth the energy of togetherness without sympathy or feeling sorry for others. Compassionate detachment allows you to love others from a distance so they may evolve at their own pace.

Today's Higher Idea: Practice compassion, love, and kindness every day to inspire others to see beyond their suffering. We are not here to stay in our Suffering self. We are here to remember that we are more powerful than the pain we have experienced.

Higher Idea #46 Breathe in Gratitude

After you have crossed the bridge of Forgiveness, the vibration of Gratitude will open the gates to fully living in the Freedom Frequency. The vibration of gratitude will instantly create positive shifts in your life. When you choose to see the gifts in every moment and be grateful for the life lessons others bring, you are living above the line.

Some take for granted the good that is already present in their lives. If you've already brought forth a practice of gratitude into your life—in which you acknowledge and are thankful for everything you receive, no matter what it is—then you have transformed a powerful Forgotten Angel into a Remembered Angel.

We have so much for which to be grateful. Look at the amazing planet we live on. The energy of gratitude has the power to shift your perspective completely and to pop you out of a fearful mind. Any time you are in the pit of fear or have lost your faith in the Universe, ask the question, "What am I grateful for?" Continue to reflect on this question until you receive an answer.

Showing others how grateful you are for their kindness, generosity, time, or energy is important. You can uplift someone and change her or his state of mind instantly just by looking them in the eye, saying, "Thank you," and letting them know three reasons why you're grateful for having her or him in your life. This is one of the biggest gifts that we can give our loved ones, coworkers, family, or friends.

Today's Higher Idea: The gratitude vibration will spiral you up into the Freedom Frequency faster than you can say, "I am living above the line." Write in your journal ten things for which you are grateful, and then share them with the ones you love. When faced with adversity ask, "How can I benefit from this?" or "What am I to learn from this?"

Higher Idea #47 Learn to Hold Space for Others

Did you know that you have the ability to stand in the fire of another's anger and not be affected by it in a negative way? I am not saying you must tolerate negative behaviour—just that you don't have to let it affect you. Ultimately, self-love is not allowing the behaviour of others to take away the love and peace that is you.

If you have attended any workshops, you will know that "holding space" is the ability to sit in the energy of someone's anger, sadness, or fear while remaining calm, centered, and compassionately detached. Holding space is the art of being an observer or witness to another as they shift in consciousness and experience the gifts that vulnerability brings. When you hold space for another, especially in intimate relationships, it can be a game changer. Your beloved will feel safe and supported; she/he will trust you completely because they know you will not judge them, which will open them up to expressing their deepest truth. Your beloved can now talk about whatever mistakes they want to make right, share their emotional pain, and discover their own capacity to solve problems.

The most powerful resolution to conflict is showing appreciation for the divine nature within the Divine being before you. You know and trust that your beloved is not their emotions; they are only processing their experience in the only way they know how. They may be living unconsciously in fear, and we must have compassion for all those still living below the line. This is not to say we must tolerate abuse. Holding space means you are not contributing to or engaging in the emotional pollution. While holding space, you remember that underneath all anger is sadness, and underneath all sadness is fear. Underneath fear is where your Forgotten Angels are who have the power to spiral you up above the line.

When you hold the energy of compassion and someone feels angry, you have the power to stand unaffected by anyone's emotional rage. It's a skill that can be learned. When you resonate in the Freedom Frequency you can see the projected negative energy move *around* you instead of *through* you.

Holding space allows others to open up, to feel vulnerable, and then stabilize as they discover answers to their questions. You're not there to give advice or your opinion. You're only there to emit love from your heart and consciously listen to the journey of another. Developing your ability to *hold the space* in everyday life allows you to be sensitive and listen consciously to anyone who is in your presence.

Holding space also means understanding that whatever someone is expressing about how they *feel* about you or anything else, is their truth, not yours. Their Fallen Angels are expressing themselves, and Fallen Angels love to blame. You're allowing an important process to take place as powerful energies are released from their physical body that would otherwise be harmful if kept suppressed.

Today's Higher Idea: The next time you experience someone arguing, take a moment and recognize the Divine light within. Just know she/he is verbally releasing toxic energy from their body. Practice observing others with curiosity and compassion; it is a powerful skill. If you practice this skill, you'll be able to stand in the midst of chaos and not be affected in a negative way by those around you. This takes time and patience, but peace within any situation can be truly experienced by anyone if the desire is there. Recognize the Goddess/God within you and others.

Higher Idea #48 Honour Mother Earth

We have explored how we relate to others and ourselves, but this chapter would not be complete if we did not explore our relationship with the Earth. Many of us walk, drive, and build our homes on this beautiful planet without realizing she is a conscious and living being. Without her life support system, we couldn't survive. We're interrelated and can no longer take the planet we live on for granted.

Mother Earth feeds, shades, gives us warmth, protects, and provides us with an abundance of natural resources. We need to remind ourselves to become consciously aware of the responsibility we have for conserving the natural world.

We all have a natural frequency that resonates with the Earth's, which is harmonic in nature. There are natural frequencies and man-made frequencies. Man-made frequencies such as microwaves, TVs, and computers create disharmony in the body. Mother Earth has a natural frequency that will immediately harmonize with your frequency. Only when you are vibrating in harmony can you create a healthy body and a healthy life.

Surround yourself with the natural frequencies of the Earth as often as you can by walking in nature or meditating under trees, even if they're in your backyard. Simply acknowledge and show appreciation for the natural beauty that surrounds you.

In ancient times, prior to God-worship, there was a culture that honoured the Earth. It was a time of the Goddess, when the feminine principle was cherished for its life-giving qualities. Feminine energy is rising again and as men and women embrace these nurturing inner qualities, we can all ride the wave to *enlightened love*. Once we achieve internal appreciation, we learn to extend our appreciation to the external world. As we uplift our lives, we can teach our young ones to live by the same principles.

Mother Earth does not need saving, she knows how to take care of herself. She can cleanse herself any time. Our earth is multi-dimensional, just like *you*. If there is any saving to be done, it is to save yourself. She has offered herself as a school for your learning. She needs to be respected. She is aware of those who love her and those who do not. If you make the time to connect and send love into the crystalline core of Mother Earth, she will make sure you are always guided to a safe place in times of destruction. The next time you are walking in nature, take time to feel your connection to the water, trees, and life around you. Mother Earth is always listening. She is waiting to nurture you.

Some simple contributions we can all make to honour our beautiful planet include:

- Join, support, or create a conscious movement that expands our global and social responsibility.
- Invest only in products or companies that honour all of life.
- Use natural products instead of chemicals.
- Eat natural or organic foods instead of chemically sprayed foods.
- Use natural fertilizers.

- Take part in an Earth Ceremony of Appreciation or global meditation.
- Send loving thoughts to the crystalline core of Mother Earth when you meditate.
- Walk on the grass with bare feet as often as you can.
- Hug trees! They are much more than your physical eyes can see.

Native cultures recognize the spirit in all living things. Aboriginal cultures have always maintained a deep connection to the Earth. They have much to teach us when we are ready to learn. Let's remember our native ancestors, the ones who were here first, and listen to the beat of their drums. Let's unite with our native brothers and sisters of the Earth, with the aboriginal spirit that connects us in our vision quest for freedom.

Today's Higher Idea: Drop your ego and hug a tree.

Chapter Five
Express Your Truth

Are you afraid of expressing your curiosity, interests, or deepest desires? What about expressing your needs or wants? It's not uncommon for us to hold back self-expression for fear of being judged, laughed at, or criticized. Many of us hold back our truths because we are afraid to express the deepest parts of ourselves. This fear can leave us feeling powerless and dissatisfied, and it can impair our ability to connect meaningfully with others.

This chapter will focus on ways of creating healthy self-expression through the power of *relating*. The evolution of the Self involves re-establishing your relationship with the internal worlds of your mind, emotions, and spirituality, and deepening your soul's interactions with others. Relationships are as much about valuing yourself as they are about reaching out and helping others.

Spirituality is a journey toward truth and aligning with Source energy. It is not about finding yourself as much as it is about remembering the truth of who you are. Expressing your truth can be uncomfortable at first. When you learn how to express your truth from a place of love, compassion, and appreciation for what is showing up and seeking to be expressed, the uncomfortable energy in your body will begin to shift into a greater sense of relief and, eventually, inner peace.

Higher Idea #49 Live in Truth

We have collectively created a fear of looking honestly at ourselves, and this fear causes us to deny truth. We therefore will argue our right to live in limitation, pain, and suffering. For example, when someone suggests a better way of doing things, we get defensive and argue for the things that currently limit us. We have learned to deceive others and especially ourselves through lifetimes of observation and learned behaviour from a world suffering with low self-esteem or no sense of self.

How can you raise your vibration and live in the Freedom Frequency? The answer is simple: Truth! The more truth you bring into your life, the lighter you become. Lies are wrought with heavy energies, especially when we lie to ourselves. Many of us are afraid of truth; however, it's the quality of truth that marks those who are spiritually wealthy and noble. Truth allows us to open our eyes, remove the veil of denial, and untangle the illusions of our life.

Lack of truth has consequences. Lies are like scissors that cut away the attraction cords of any relationship. Every act that is not built on truth will lead to self-sabotage. When you are vibrating in truth, you can no longer speak lies or manipulate others.

Truth asks you to get real with *what is so*. The journey toward truth means acknowledging and feeling any untruths hidden within your mind. The path to freedom is found by moving through the frequency of fear so you can make the distinctions between what is illusion (lies we tell ourselves) and what is truth.

To create a world where love, trust, and intimacy blossom we are being called to end the deception within our own homes. We no longer need to impress others or misrepresent our life in order to look good. Authenticity is sexy, it is cool, it is hip, and it is the new truth. You can learn to tell the truth with an air of ease and grace. As you make the choice to express yourself authentically, you bring forth freedom. Reclaim your power by making a choice to live in truth.

Today's Higher Idea: What truths are you ready to express? The truth about how you feel in your relationship or how you feel about the path you are on? Identify with your Pretender self (we all have one) and tune into whether this self is in control of your life. Are you living a lie? How often do you lie to yourself and others? Who are you pretending to be? Observe without judgment. Be kind to yourself as new insights surface.

Higher Idea #50 Rise Up from Conflict

One of the most powerful books I have read was <u>Nonviolent Communication</u> by Marshall B. Rosenberg. He shows us how to express our feelings and needs from a giving heart and connect to our compassionate nature when communicating.

Many of us have not been taught how to express what we feel or need and therefore fall into old behaviour patterns, often mimicking the dysfunctional way our fathers and mothers related to each other.

Conflict in your outer world is a reflection of conflict within your own mind. The conflict between the *ego* and your *soul* is the only battle that creates hell in any and all relationships. When you are afraid of conflict you are afraid to face your own mind, your own Fallen Angels who interpret others and life experiences as wrong and bad.

When you are in conflict you are in your head, and you are being asked to drop down into your heart and into your body to *feel* the energy that is alive inside you. Conflict has a way of revealing the truth of where you are mentally, emotionally, and spiritually.

The root of conflict is *fear*—fear of being threatened, not being appreciated, understood, valued, or acknowledged for the man/woman you believe you are. If you have conflict in your relationships, it means you are afraid of each other. Afraid to see and talk about the elephant in the room.

One of the biggest fears related to conflict is the *fear of being seen.* Being seen for all your perceived mistakes or failures, being seen in your vulnerability, or being found out that you have been pretending to be someone you are not. Fear of being seen brings forth the fear of being found out for not being as educated as others, for the wrongful acts of our past, or for not being as strong as you may pretend to be.

Today's Higher Idea: If you rise out of conflict, this requires you to stop being afraid of your emotions, of each other, and to embrace our own vulnerability. You are being called to communicate from a deeper place. Say out loud, "I now choose to release my fear of conflict. I now choose to have a learning attitude about myself and others."

Higher Idea #51 Cultivating the Right Attitude

Are you a complainer? When you complain or have a negative attitude about life, you are really complaining about what you have created and your inability to cope with it. Buddhist philosophy identifies eight signposts to freedom. One signpost is *right* attitude or thought, which means to become consciously aware of your thoughts and start thinking from the highest point of view. When you complain, you have been feeding your mind garbage. What good does this do you?

Your attitude is important, and having an above the line attitude means releasing the garbage in your mind. When you move out of the realm of "I can't" to the realm of "I can", you are releasing the inner Fallen Angel that is saying, "I won't." Your mind will create resistance to thinking higher thoughts about your experience because it has been programmed to disapprove of yourself and others.

Your Divine intelligence breathes in the positive essence of your creations as you move out of the worlds of right, wrong, good, or bad and into accepting the neutrality of life's Divine order. Happiness lives inside you, and you can choose to connect to this higher vibration, even if your bills are not being paid or when you are not getting what you want. Complaining robs you of your happiness.

We are all capable of moving through suffering and pain by releasing the negative energetic charge we have associated with certain moments. You'll know you've transformed the emotional body when you can say, "I now choose to approve of myself and others and live above the line in the Freedom Frequency of life." With this attitude, you will be able to look back on your past with a smile and create heaven in your life.

Choose today to have an optimistic view about life. To have an attitude of knowing that things are going to turn around. To believe that this present moment is a blessing in disguise. To see that this is just a moment within a trillion moments of your life and you are preparing yourself to live in the Freedom Frequency of life.

Today's Higher Idea: Share with someone you love and express the words, "I have a learning attitude."

Higher Idea #52 Spiral Up in Your Thoughts

There is nothing that limits you or keeps you in a state of doubt except your thoughts. Your mental power is highly creative. You are either operating from a fear-based mind or your Divine Mind. Thoughts can either destroy or uplift you. Everything you taste, touch, feel, or smell was first created in your mind through thought. Your thoughts are often expressed through the words you speak, and if you believe what you say to be true, then the energy behind your words will cause you to act.

Many of us walk the same path everyday doing habitual things but expecting our lives to change. For change to occur in your outer world, you must first *think and feel the change* in your inner world. Whatever you focus your thoughts on is what you will experience, whether you like it or not. When you recognize that it's the subconscious mind that dictates your experiences, you realize how important it is to understand and restructure the controlling thoughts that are manifesting the world you see.

Much of the time we're unaware that the thoughts we have are actually images. If I told you not to think about a red Lamborghini, (this is my inner Race Car Driver speaking) what would happen? Your mind would immediately picture a red Lamborghini. These pictures run through our minds at the speed of light, and it's only when we become consciously aware of our mental realm that we discover the inner movies we create.

You may appear outwardly nice to others, but what thoughts do you have when their backs are turned? Remember, we are all energetically connected. If others are spiritually attuned, they can also read your energy vibrations and the truth behind your words. How you feel about someone doesn't have to be expressed verbally for them to know your vibration. Thoughts alone are easy to read when you have awareness. How you truly think about others will eventually make itself known, and you will experience the effects of that thinking such as: if you send loving or compassionate thoughts you will receive more love in your life and if you are sending out hateful and envious thoughts you will attract more hate and create negative experiences.

It is good practice to be aware of your thoughts regarding others, but even more importantly, to be aware of how you think about yourself. Negative thoughts about yourself or others such as "I don't deserve to be loved" or "He's a loser" are destructive. The thoughts you have about others mirror exactly how you feel about yourself. Fear-based thoughts cannot continue if you want a better life. If you're thinking too much, you're cutting yourself off from connecting to your heart. Less thinking and more feeling is the key.

When life is challenging, you may experience setbacks and delays in making your dreams come true. You may lose faith in yourself or question the journey you are on. Your doubt can become overwhelming. Your fear-ridden mind can take you on a wild and uncomfortable ride. Thoughts like "I can't do this" or "What was I thinking?" or "I'm not smart enough" cloud your better judgment. When you are in your fear-based mind you doubt your capabilities, talents, and skills. This doesn't sound like fun, does it? Now is the time to spiral UP above the line which means becoming aware of how you choose to think about yourself and your life.

Your thoughts will become conflicting when you consciously or unconsciously surround yourself with negative images every day. These images enter your mind through television, music, movies, and even reading the newspaper. Your thoughts are energetic, so it's important to reduce the amount of negativity in your life by making conscious choices and asking yourself, "Is what I'm doing now going to benefit my life?" If what you're doing doesn't make you a better Divine being, then why bother? Find something that will expand your mind and uplift your life.

You create reality by what you choose to think and what you choose to believe in. That's how powerful your thinking is. You can have either fearful thoughts or freedom thoughts. The more aware you are of what you're thinking in the present moment, the more choice you have to change your thoughts and how you feel about your life.

Today's Higher Idea: You have a choice about which mind you want to operate from—a Fear-based mind or your Divine Mind. To connect to your Divine Mind and uplift your mood, listen to Baroque music. The vibration of Baroque music stimulates whole brain thinking, enhances creativity, and at the same time calms your mind.

Higher Idea #53 Spiral Up in Your Words

Do words have the power to affect your health and well-being? The answer is: Yes. Words have a lot of energy behind them, and they can affect you positively or negatively. Words are sound vibrations, and they carry either a positive or negative charge which is fuelled by your intention or the emotional energy you associate with the word. For instance, the word *love* carries a high frequency and has the power to heal and transmute all negativity. However, if you have fear associated with the word love, you will create a barrier to experiencing the profound freedom *love* brings.

Dr. Masaru Emoto, a Japanese visionary, researcher, and the author of *The Hidden Messages in Water*, (see Resources section) provided evidence that our thoughts and words affect the molecular structure of water. Water crystals exposed to verbal insults became black and distorted. Water crystals exposed to loving and compassionate thoughts and words produced beautiful crystal configurations. Dr. Emoto has shown us through his extraordinary work that water takes on the energy vibrations of the environment. Since our physical bodies are made of 70 percent water, we are affected in the same way. Loving, encouraging, compassionate words produce harmonic energy in our bodies. Insults, negativity, and listening to harsh music produce disharmonic energy and will lower your vibration.

It's important to become aware of the words you speak and the words to which you listen. It is also important to become clear about the intent or motivation behind those words. Are they driven by ego which is fear-based, or are you expressing yourself from the heart, from a caring perspective? One word or term expressed repeatedly with negative intention can manifest dire consequences. The Law of Attraction states that whatever you focus on, you create more of in the physical realm. For example, there is currently so much discussion about breast cancer in the world and women are experiencing an alarming increase in the manifestation of it. We have given this word so much power. What if the cure was as simple as becoming aware of our own inner Cancer self, the Fallen Angel that knows it is not loved? What if we collectively held space and connected to our Cancer selves and dissolved the seed within that carries the negative energetic charge? We could say, "I now take my power back." If we could dissolve anger, disapproval, or any negative emotion completely with this process, then what if this higher idea could dissolve dis-ease, the lack of ease in the body? Could we dissolve the negative charge of this word, the word *cancer,* and release the fear associated with it? As long as we have fear wrapped around that word, we will create the exact thing we don't want. I believe *self-love* can cure anything, especially when it has been proven that loving thoughts and words have the power to heal and create inner beauty. Now we can let our wings expand and see that heaven is right here, right now.

If you speak with the intent to manipulate, judge, criticize, or deceive others, you will experience the results of those words. If you are ever having a bad day, check your state of mind to see whether you have projected any negativity toward anyone. What's coming back to you is a result of your own thinking. Remember, you get back what you put out. In order to experience a transformation in your mental dimensions, you must change your idea of what communication is. You can use words either to help you in the creation process or as destructive weapons that will boomerang right back at you.

Today's Higher Idea: The vibration of your words can either spiral you down toward destruction or spiral you up to living above the line. If you are ready to raise your vibration and live in the Freedom Frequency, start today and spiral up in your *words* by practicing the following higher expressions.

- I am grateful for everything in my life.
- I am living with ease and grace.
- I love and appreciate myself as I am.
- The more I love myself, the more love I have to give others.
- I am now attracting loving and meaningful relationships.
- I love my soul-inspiring business, and I am richly rewarded creatively and financially.
- I always communicate clearly and effectively.
- I am always in the right place at the right time.
- This is an abundant universe and there is plenty for all.
- I am prosperous and I share my wealth with others.
- I always make time to play and enjoy myself.
- I recognize time is fluid, and I have plenty of time for everything.

And So It Is!

Higher Idea #54 Spiral Up in Your Actions

Do you ever question the motivation behind your actions? Are you doing things to make yourself look good, or are you actually assisting others to achieve their dreams?

Thought is the first level of creation. It's followed by feelings, which we express in both words and actions. Everything you say is an expression of thought or feeling followed with action. You can talk all you want about love. It will be your actions that will be the true expression of your heart.

You are taking action from either one of two realms of consciousness—fear-based action or soul-inspired action. Fear-based actions are when you allow ego to dominate, like approaching a situation from a place of control, greed, or seeking revenge because you believe someone did you wrong. If you take action from a place of fear, need, or desperation you are not in alignment with freedom. Instead, you'll experience the consequences of those fear-based actions.

To shift into higher vibrations of freedom, I suggest you only take inspired action. At the core of inspired action is spirit, your Divine Mind. When you take action from this place, your results are always rewarding and deeply fulfilling.

Recognize the power behind your thoughts, words, and actions. If you lie, others will be deceitful with you. If you cheat others, someone else will cheat you. If you hate, you will only see a hateful world and you will draw that negative energy to yourself, all the while wondering why things seem to be going wrong. That's how powerful you truly are. Whatever you think and believe is what you experience. Every cause has an effect, and every choice has consequences you must face.

Today's Higher Idea: Expand your awareness of every action you take, and then connect to your Observer Self. Can you rewind the movie of your life and identify where you took fear-based action and when you took inspired action? Observe yourself without judgment.

Higher Idea #55 See Others as Divine Messengers

I believe everyone is playing a role in your life for a higher purpose. You are the creator of your life and have attracted every man or woman who has crossed your path for a reason. You will meet many souls who are Divine messengers. These beautiful souls will create tremendous and painful acts just to remind you to *feel* again, to open your heart again, and to remind you to connect with your Fallen Angels, so they can be released and integrated into light.

Divine beings and circumstances seem to miraculously appear just at the right moment to teach you who you are, how you are thinking, and what you believe. You've created everyone to assist you with the choices you have made. If you are meant to learn about love, you may attract others who are not loving so you can learn how to be compassionate and understanding and to embody forgiveness. If you want to attract a partner who loves and accepts you for who you are, you may have to go through a few relationships to prepare you mentally, emotionally, and spiritually. Every event and circumstance offers a powerful learning opportunity.

The mothers and fathers who may not show love, the boss who is unappreciative, the men who use or abuse you, or the women who disrespect you—they're all there to remind you of where you are vibrating and to show you how much you are not loving or respecting yourself. Learn to see everyone as an angel in disguise and listen to her or his message of truth. Everyone is here to empower you to let go of who you are *not*, so you can embrace who you are.

If you're not enjoying where you are in life, it's up to you to change it. You may start by asking yourself the question, "How did I get myself here?" Every experience happens for a reason, yet we often don't realize this until later in life.

Everyone you meet is a Divine messenger, an *earth angel,* who is reminding you of why you came to this planet in the first place. When you have a high degree of willingness to learn, you can explore issues with a greater depth of understanding of all involved. When you see others as angels in your life, you are less likely to create conflict.

Today's Higher Idea: See everyone you meet as an *earth angel* who is here to give you a message and remind you of where you are vibrating in life. Everyone is a mirror reflection of you.

Higher Idea #56 Heart to Heart Communication

Heart to heart communication is a wonderful way to practice raising your vibration and infusing love into any relationship. Through heart to heart communication you have an opportunity to learn how to respond to others instead of reacting or blaming. Remember, underneath all conflict is a need to be heard, appreciated, and understood.

Heart to heart communication is a great practice, especially if a relationship is in a power struggle phase. If you believe you are losing your identity, your inner Fallen Angels will create separation via blame and focus on the perceived flaws or faults in your partner. If your partner doesn't change into the man/woman you want him/her to be, you may feel frustrated because your efforts to "improve" him/her aren't being appreciated. Any form of conversation from this state of mind may generate a sense of failure that will likely cause you to start putting up walls of resistance. This is an unconscious relationship pattern that will only transform into something meaningful when each man/woman becomes accountable for how he/she feels and responsible for his/her own actions and behaviours.

This style of communicating offers each Divine being an opportunity to express herself/himself eye to eye, face to face, and soul to soul. There are no demands, only requests. You begin statements with, "I am feeling…", "What I am afraid of is…", "What makes me feel this way is…", "My life lesson is…", "What I appreciate about you is…", "What I am thankful for is…"

By sharing how you feel and admitting that your unloving actions or behaviours originate from a place of fear and no longer serve the relationship, you open yourself up to having an authentic conversation. There is no blame, guilt, or judgment here because you can see how you've contributed to the situation for your own evolution of Self.

Heart to heart communication is about getting out of your head (thinking) and being fully present (in your body) with the one sitting across from you. When you offer direct eye contact and choose to observe without judgment, you can truly see that underneath all perceived negative emotions and fear, there sits a Divine being. How blessed are you! When the one you are with feels heard, appreciated, and understood, her or his negative (fear-based) behaviour begins to dissolve.

Conscious relationships are developed when you practice living from your heart and end the blame game. You no longer focus on changing your partner or pointing out faults. Instead, you focus on doing whatever it takes to empower each other. To empower yourself you will be asked to dissolve your own heart wall, raise your own vibration from fear to love, and have a learning attitude about your partner. This takes practice and patience. Your desire to evolve, live above the line, and live a heart-centered life will inspire you.

Heart to heart communication is about getting real with how you feel and what it is you need. Expressing your feelings can sometimes feel painful because you may be reminded of past failures, tragedies, or perceived wrongdoings. Do not allow any moment of life's experiences to keep you down. You are much greater than a *moment*. As you commit to spiralling out of the lower vibrations of energy and dissolving the negative charge, life will open new doors of possibilities.

We can either have soulful moments or ego hours. The choice is yours. You will know that the ego has arrived when the voice in your head tells you how wrong or bad your spouse/partner is, and you feel the urge to either fight or flee. A soul moment is when you can sit, breathe, and just BE with the sensations in your body and express what you are afraid of. Your vulnerability is the gateway to self-empowerment and enlightenment.

When you are open to listening and learning, you stop taking things personally. Hurtful words expressed reflect how that woman/man feels about herself/himself. The more you practice heart to heart communication, the more happiness and harmony you will bring into your relationships. When there is a foundation of respect and self-love, you have the power to dissolve conflict and arguments completely.

Today's Higher Idea: Practice living from your heart by putting your hand on your heart and breathing into your heart for 5 minutes. Say to yourself, "*I am releasing all fear wrapped around the idea of communicating my feelings and needs. I am now open to listening to the feelings and needs of my beloved.*" Remember, what you most want from others is sometimes the exact thing that you have not been able to give.

Higher Idea #57 Allow Others to Be Right

Is being *right* working for you? Having to be right all the time is a controlling behaviour. It can lead to power struggles, which ultimately create walls of resistance between you and the ones you love or respect.

Often, we get so caught up in our need to feel vindicated or understood that we take the long route to resolving conflict. Feuds can last for days or lifetimes, when arguments could have been turned around in moments with compassion and understanding. When you let go of the belief that you need to defend, fight, or argue in order to be heard, you begin to spiral up into the realm of conscious relationships.

When you connect to your Divine Mind you become the observer instead of the one who judges self or another. When you seek to educate yourself and learn how to dive into conflict without taking anything personally you make a quantum leap in your evolution of Self. This is a journey and takes much practice.

Others are in your life to challenge your Fallen Angels so you can become aware of how much control these inner selves have in your life. Rising up out of conflict, especially in intimate relationships, is having the courage to face your beloved, look her/him in the eye, and share how you *feel, express what you need, and what you are afraid of.* Here you have the opportunity to step into agreement and see the soul, the divinity that stands before you. When someone agrees with you, how do you feel? Happy right? Exactly! You have the power to restore harmony and bring joy into others' lives with your kind words and kind actions.

If you want to create deeper connections with your partner or loved ones, you need to seek agreement and allow others to be right. You can always find ways to agree on things. Allowing others to be right releases tension and stress and shows you have a learning attitude.

Today's Higher Idea: Having to be *right* takes up so much energy. If you are feeling exhausted maybe it is a sign to let go of your righteousness. You learn powerful life lessons in every relationship no matter if they are in your life for a reason, a season, or lifetime. Next time you are communicating, seek agreement. You can say, "I agree. You are absolutely right!"

Higher Idea #58 Create Soul Connections

Have you ever noticed that if you focus on how bad your relationship is, it just gets worse? The more negative attention you give anything, the more you create what you do not want. Your relationships will greatly improve if you choose to see your beloved or partner as a *soul* instead of the "personality" that makes you mad or frustrated. When you focus on the things that make the relationship fulfilling, you will experience just that—a fulfilling relationship. Use your imagination and the power of your mind to visualize greater possibilities and positive outcomes. Instead of expecting the worst, first create the best possible scenario in your mind, and then watch your relationships transform.

The goal when communicating with others is to *relate* rather than react. Relationships are an opportunity to seek understanding about yourself. If you feel you are not being understood, then you are being asked to communicate more effectively. You are being asked to go deeper into truth. When you make a conscious choice to stop the abusive pattern of yelling, shoving, swearing, or raising your voice at another, you raise your vibration to that of self-maturity and emotional mastery.

If you have painful experiences when communicating with your partner, family members, or other significant ones in your life, then maybe it's time to ask yourself, "Do the feelings I have right now remind me of how I felt when I was young? What's the lesson here?" Maybe it's time for you to say something kind and meaningful to those who trigger a negative energetic charge. Maybe your soul is calling you to step *first* into love. Surprise others with kindness—like a hug, an apology, or thoughtful words. You have the power to weaken all negative influences just by being kind, thoughtful, and loving. The key is to be open and honest about who you are, and not to blame others for how you feel.

When you stop blaming others for how you feel or for a situation gone wrong, you will transform your relationship into something you have always wanted. Admit how you could have contributed to the problem at hand, and now focus on how you both can create a win-win. If an apology is required, apologize because you value your relationship more than your ego. This practice will help you to explore issues or problems honestly with knowledge, understanding, and love. On the other side of conflict is a wonderful gift awaiting you—an enriched relationship.

Releasing the fears surrounding communication allows for change. If an argument ensues, know that it is designed to bring forth clarity. The *Divine Mind Conversation* is a powerful technique that when practiced often can end an argument in five minutes. If two souls are arguing for more than fifteen minutes, it means a Fallen Angel has taken over and they have become puppets on a string. Such an argument can only stop when the voice of soul love is heard from within. Every argument is actually a misunderstanding about two souls' needs not being met.

When we learn to ask the right questions, let go of making assumptions, and allow for others' points of view to be expressed, we become empowered. Our energy sphere resonates in the world of understanding and compassion.

Mutual agreements must be made and followed through for future communications to be more harmonious. Issues that arise force us to find solutions that will help us evolve to the next level of being. The next time an issue is put on the table, take a deep breath and ask your Brilliant Self to give you the power to move through any uncomfortable situation that might arise. You'll experience moments of soul connection instead of two egos battling it out for hours to see who will win. The moment you realize your behaviour is hurtful, embarrassing, or damaging to the ones around you, you need to stop and do whatever it takes to get your thought vibrations above the line.

Never take out your rage on another divine being or animal. If you need to yell, *yell at your Angry self,* for it is this *self* that carries the seed of your crisis. Releasing this energy will spiral you up into the Freedom Frequency. If you need to vent the uncomfortable energy in the Fear Frequency, redirect your energy to an inanimate object such as a couch or pillow. Kneeling down and beating up your couch or pillow instead of projecting it onto a loved one helps to vent frustration and allows for a much healthier release (see Resources section).

Taking responsibility for how you feel shows maturity and the determination to become a better Divine being. Do not be afraid to address issues. Issues are the catalysts for correcting behaviour patterns and releasing any fear that's holding you back from experiencing what you need or desire. Trust that you have the power to move through any problem or any challenge that life gives you.

If conflict gets out of control and you suffer emotional, mental, or physical abuse, you must ask yourself, "What action do I need to take to change my experience?" or "Who am I to allow this behaviour to be in my life?" or "How can I disengage and not contribute to this unhealthy cycle?" If someone is mean, rude, or constantly crushing your spirit, they are letting you know it is time for you to claim your power back. Never stay where you're not appreciated. You always have a choice to seek out others who will support and respect you rather than limit or hurt you.

Happiness within relationships comes from embracing, embodying, and nurturing the Happy Self. The more you and your partner make the relationship a priority, the more you create a soul connection. You create soul connections when you end the game of *being right* or blaming others for your own life experiences. Instead, you can lead by example, sharing the truth about your current vibration and what you want to experience in greater abundance. In this way, you tap into your own spiritual power and create each day in a vibration of appreciation and love.

Soul connections are created when you open up to higher self-expression. The vibration of *pleasure* will allow a higher self-expression of love for self and others to integrate much quicker. Any time you practice saying positive statements, a higher idea is to bring the energy of *pleasure*, calmness, and sincerity into your expression. The more you do the inner work of creating a beautiful mind and expanding your heart, the more you begin to express new possibilities which will attract others into your life who want to support you in your cause.

Today's Higher Idea: Every day is a new day. Listen to your heart and connect to the heart of another. Make every effort to listen to others' points of view instead of making a judgment or creating wrongness. If you do not understand, seek to learn more.

Higher Idea #59 Upgrade Your Sphere of Influence

Do others in your life inspire and encourage you to live above the line in the *Freedom Frequency*? Raising your vibration out of the worlds of suffering, pain, illness, or lack involves changing your environment, which may include changing some of those with whom you associate.

If you're wondering why certain beings are in your life, it's because your vibration resonates with their vibrations. If you want to attract different beings into your life, you have the power to direct your vibrations to a higher frequency. Remember, those who are successful associate with others who are successful and who are passionate about life. If you want to learn how to become prosperous, you'll advance further if you associate with those who are prosperous. If you want more peace in your life, then I suggest you associate with those who have already obtained peace of mind.

Everyone you meet and connect with in life mirrors your state of mind. For example, your brain transmits thought vibrations that are picked up by others who are transmitting the same frequency. If you have low self-esteem, you only attract others with low self-esteem. As your state of mind spirals up, so do your relationships, and you may recognize that others who you once thought of as friends, may not have your best interests at heart.

Your surroundings change the moment you project a cord of intention to a higher frequency in which you desire to vibrate. As you spiral up, you may find that many others in your present sphere may not be ready to leave the comfort zone of the frequency in which they vibrate. There is usually a grieving process as you let go of those who no longer support your journey. Setting others free with love is the most honouring way of ending any relationship. Remember, everyone is growing at her or his own pace.

Today's Higher Idea: Start connecting with others who talk about higher ideas instead of those who just talk about others. When you have the courage to say goodbye and turn towards the direction of your dreams you will discover many amazing souls who want to say hi!

Chapter Six
Give Your Imagination a Purpose

Living above the line requires the application of one of your biggest gifts—*your imagination.* The power of your imagination can change your circumstances drastically. It can transform your environment, attract wealth and meaningful relationships into your life, and improve your health dramatically. When you expand your awareness, direct your mental and emotional energy toward a greater reality, and transform your Forgotten Angels into Remembered Angels, you align with the Creator within. Here you see yourself as whole, the complete You!

Unfortunately, as we move into adulthood, our imagination is often dormant. Learning to utilize the powerful gift of your *imagination* will give you the capacity to transform your life.

This chapter will show you how your imagination is the gateway to your invisible worlds—your emotional, mental, and spiritual dimensions. I will show you how the vision you hold in your heart is what guides you to your destiny. It's the reason you are here on this planet in the first place! And I will show you that the best way to connect with your inner Fallen or Forgotten Angels is through the power of your imagination. Using your imagination, you can tap into internal forces that will give you the power to heal your body, overcome fear, change behaviour patterns, and bring forth hidden talents. Your imagination opens the door to the inner worlds of your subconscious and Divine Mind, which will allow you to bring forth the power of insight, higher vision, and creative expression.

Higher Idea #60 A Great Life Starts with a Vision

The vision of your life is not necessarily about creating a career or how you are going to make money. That will continue to be expressed as you gain clarity on the woman/man you are here to *BE*. What matters most is how you feel and see yourself, now and in the future. When you have the courage to redirect your focus from outside yourself and explore your invisible worlds, which are very much *alive* inside you, a whole new perspective on life begins to take shape.

The more clarity you have about who you want to *be* and how you want to live, the more ideas and opportunities you attract. If all you see is a void in your future, then you will create more struggle than necessary. It would be a higher idea to picture your own prophecy that is filled with a grander vision for yourself and your family.

If you do not determine the path for yourself, then there is the possibility of being swept away into another's reality, which may not be in alignment with your dreams and vision. Creating a vision will give you a strong focus and desire, which will prevent your fear from discouraging you. Trust that once you have a vision of where you want to go, you will meet others along the path who will support and encourage you.

Your mind is vast and powerful, and when you learn how to direct its energies with your imagination and have them work *for* you rather than *against* you, you will be living in the Freedom Frequency of life. For instance, you may have the desire to start your own business or write a book. Change can be overwhelming, but if you plan and organize your life with your imagination first, you can create the necessary steps and possible scenarios that create joy and attract infinite possibilities.

Be aware that your *fearful mind* may take over and attempt to create visions of something *bad* happening to you in an attempt to keep you living below the line. The Sabotaging self will attempt to distract you and create negative thoughts and images of your future, as this Fallen Angel within is designed to stay in control and keep you away from certainty and truth. Remember the forces of the universe are always *with* you. The only thing against you is You (the unresolved fear within your own mind.) As you move toward who you want to *be,* everything that is unlike it will rise up to be healed and transformed. Learning how to use your imagination in the right way is the most effective approach to shifting your vibration so you can remember your Divine power.

Every time you have images of a bleak future, and these images do not make you feel good, trust that these images and stories are mental distortions and are not true. When this happens, do whatever it takes to get yourself to a place of feeling good again.

If you are feeling frustrated or overwhelmed when course correcting your mental images, ask yourself, "What is true for me right now?" If you have resistance to visualizing your future, make that okay. If what is true for you right now is feeling powerless to change your thoughts, then let that be your truth. Let that be enough. Take a deep breath. Close your eyes again and begin to cultivate images that make you feel good about YOU! For example, maybe you are visualizing yourself at a party and others are smiling and welcoming you as you walk into the room. You feel respected and everyone enjoys being in your presence.

We are also on this earth to create a new vision for us all. If we collectively focus on a vision of connection, unity, and love for all, we have the power to birth a new reality. Our hearts are calling for all of us to step into a higher vision and remember our deepest truth. The more clarity and insights you have about who you are and the power that resonates in every cell of your being, the more your vision expands, giving you the gift of freedom.

Today's Higher Idea: Take 10 minutes every day and visualize the best life you want to experience as if it is happening right now.

Higher Idea #61 Practice Creative Visualization

Have you ever felt so close to realizing your dream, and then for some reason, everything fell apart to the point where it seemed as if you were at the opposite end of what you wanted to create? You will experience great resistance to change if your mind is constantly creating fearful mental images. Your Fallen Angels will resist everything you want until they are gently persuaded and come into agreement with what you desire. Your subconscious mind is here to serve you. However, your subconscious mind has been programmed to live in the fear frequency. Now it is up to you to become aware of and activate the power that is within.

Your heart and mind must come to agreement on whatever it is you desire. Since your Fallen Angels reside in your subconscious, and you cannot physically taste, touch, feel, hear, or see your subconscious mind, wouldn't it make sense to use your imagination so you can? Creative visualization is a powerful tool you can use to connect with hidden parts of yourself.

Here are a few examples of how you can use the power of creative visualization to empower you and make you feel a greater sense of relief.

Can't Keep My Head Above Water—When you feel this way, visualize yourself in the water; you are exhausted and can barely keep your head above the water's surface. Now look down into the water and release the plug. See the water level going down until there is no more water. Now you realize you were in a bathtub. Feel the relief.

Feel Stuck in Life—When you feel this way, visualize yourself stuck in the mud. Now see yourself clutching onto a branch and pulling yourself out. See yourself standing on solid ground. Take a deep breath and walk forward. Feel the freedom you have in moving forward with ease now.

Heavy Burden on Shoulders—When you feel this way, visualize yourself with a heavy backpack full of bricks. Now see yourself unhooking the backpack and letting it fall to the ground. Feel how much lighter you are. Take three slow deep-belly breaths and exhale slowly.

Feeling Pressure—You may feel as if you have a vice grip on your head or someone is pushing down on you. Close your eyes and see yourself sitting on a chair with a vice grip on your head. See yourself releasing the vice grip and taking it off your head. Feel the release. This works!

If you feel someone is pushing you down, turn around and see who it is. Now take their hands off you and tell him or her that you are taking your power back. Stand up tall and see yourself walking forward. Now you are using your imagination *for* you instead of against you. This is your Divine power.

Today's Higher Idea: Any time you are feeling stressed, take five minutes to state how you feel using a metaphor, and then use your imagination to change the scene and empower yourself.

Higher Idea #62 Live Every Day with Intention

Are you experiencing instantaneous creations? Have you thought of someone and then the next minute they are calling you on the phone? Or you're thinking about going out for dinner to your favourite restaurant when your beloved walks in the room and asks you if you would like to go out for dinner to your favourite restaurant? Or, when your thoughts are focused on how bad life is, you stub your toe? Or the meeting you were looking forward to is cancelled? Whatever you concentrate on will expand in your reality. This is why it is so important to become conscious of the thoughts you are projecting.

Conscious or Divine intentions are defined as focused attention or giving direction to the mind about what it is you want to experience. A powerful way to tune into the *Creator* within, your Divine Mind, is to create Divine Intentions. These intentions focus you on raising your vibration and they help you clarify how you want to *feel* throughout the day. Everything you want to experience in life is based on how you want to *feel* within, such as more joy, love, respect, or appreciation. Consciously creating an intention of how you want to *feel* during the day or week would be wise and does not rely on an external outcome.

Since every day offers a new opportunity to show up and live the highest version of who you are, you can intentionally create how you want your day or week to unfold. A daily intention will direct your mind to what it is you want to create in order to experience *feel good* sensations in your body. For example, when you wake up each morning, state out loud, "With Divine Intention, I now release all negative thought projections and consciously create my day to be one of ease and grace."

Every Sunday evening before you sleep, I suggest you also create a weekly intention such as, "With Divine Intention, I now create my week to be full of energy, abundance of all good things, creative flow in my work, and to be respected and appreciated by others." Visualize and feel the difference this intention can bring into your life.

Today's Higher Idea: Whenever you feel things are not working out, go to the place of your original intention to see if it was in alignment with your values, energy, and beliefs. If not, start again and set a new intention that resonates from your heart.

Higher Idea #63 See Your Body in Optimal Health

You have the ability to transform your physical body into a higher vibration of health. I have witnessed, time and time again, how the power of love and the imagination can transform mental, emotional, and physical limitations.

I suffered with chronic back pain for many years, and at the time, the only thing my doctors recommended was a drug to numb the pain. Unfortunately, I was at a point where drugs were having no effect, so my doctor recommended back surgery. At that moment, my body signalled an alarm so loud I could not ignore it. I honour Western medicine and see the need for it in severe cases. I made the choice to find an alternative way to healing my pain and to find a health care practitioner who did not believe drugs and/or surgery were the answers to every health issue. I was also ready to test the theory of mind power in healing my body.

I began to do light exercises every day such as walking or simple stretching. I was then drawn to deepen my meditation. For years, I would only meditate on a chair, but my intuition was guiding me to sit on the floor, which I found to be extremely uncomfortable. I realized how my meditation was giving birth to an active imagination, and my Brilliant Self continually reminded me to trust the process. I could not believe how afraid I was of my own mind, of what I would find. My ego did not want me going within, so it created quite the inner drama game, putting up a huge amount of resistance. Thankfully, my devotion to my soul's calling was growing bigger than the fearful voices of my Fallen Angels, so I eventually made my way to the floor. Instead of fearing the pain, I began to breathe into it. Closing my eyes and placing my full attention on my back, my body began to show me deeper parts of myself, which I had been completely unaware of. My physical pain took on a physical form, and, as my mind's eye opened, I was shown how I could heal my pain and integrate my divine health blueprint.

I could see gold rings that were wrapped around what appeared to be long spaghetti-like cords. As my awareness expanded, I could see dozens of gold rings tightly holding these cords. I intuitively knew I was to cut them, so I began cutting the gold rings with my imaginary scissors and WOW! I could feel the pain in my back instantly releasing. The relief I felt in that moment was profound. I began to cry uncontrollably. The emotional release was exactly what I needed, and once it was complete, I imagined my body being filled with golden light. I knew Divine intelligence was transforming that area of my body. Over the next few months, any time I felt pain in my back, I would simply close my eyes and cut the rings. The intensity of my chronic back pain decreased with every session until, eventually, it was completely gone.

With further insight, I realized that the rings had symbolized the unhealthy bond I had with the man I had been married to many years earlier. I didn't realize how much resentment I had been carrying. Now I had cut myself free from a past that no longer served me.

I am happy to say that I no longer have any imaginary rings to cut, and I have completely freed myself of chronic back pain and all the illnesses I described in this book's introduction. When you honour yourself, trust in your intuition, and dare to take the journey into your subconscious mind, you will be shown the way to emotional, mental, spiritual, and physical freedom.

Pain reminds you that your body is in disharmony, and you need to immediately change your course of action. You have extraordinary capabilities to dissolve pain and to transform your physical body through the power of your imagination. Connecting to your Divine Mind, you integrate your health blueprint, which activates cellular memory, to remember the truth of who you are—*Divine perfection.*

Today's Higher Idea: Close your eyes and visualize a violet flame around your body as if you are standing in a purple bubble. You can say, "By divine intention, I now ask the violet flame to transmute all negative energy in and around my physical body. I now ask that my cellular blueprint be activated to that of divine perfection. Health is my natural state. And so it is."

Higher Idea #64 Practice Meditation

What excuse do you have that stops you from meditating? Is it, "I don't have time," or "I can't focus," or "I can't sit still," or "There are too many thoughts in my head?"

Why is it that we are willing to sit behind the wheel of a vehicle and put ourselves into the chaos of traffic, but putting ourselves into the chaos of our thoughts is too scary? If we are afraid of our minds and ourselves, we then live in fear of others and the world we live in. One of the main reasons why I teach meditation is to assist you in relinquishing the fears that are limiting you so you can see that underneath all fear is your own divinity.

Meditation is the most transformative tool I practice and teach. Every sage or prophet became such through the power of meditation. You embody what you constantly think about, so if you want to embody the higher vibrations within the Freedom Frequency, then you need to consider meditation. In meditation, you become the observer of your thoughts instead of engaging in them. Meditation is about being. Meditation connects you to your Divine Mind and to all your Forgotten Angels that embody higher intelligence.

When you meditate, you enter the theta state—deep relaxation— and learning is accelerated when you are in this trance-like state. Meditation leads the way to whole brain thinking, integrating the activity of both left and right hemispheres. This integration opens the doors of perception, allowing higher information as well as higher forms of light to fill your mind, body, and soul. Becoming more mindful of your thoughts, words, and actions will inspire you toward a higher expression of character.

If you have time to watch a thirty-minute television show, you have time to meditate. There is no right or wrong way to meditate. If you feel resistance to meditation, it's because you're afraid to discover what's in your mind. Meditation will guide you to discover the secrets to overcoming your fear.

When you meditate for long periods of time, images will appear; sometimes a sequence of images, just like a movie, will cross the screen of your mind. These images offer you guidance on your journey. It is here that you receive all the answers to your questions.

To manifest what you want in this world, you cannot just sit and wait for it. You need to take inspired action! Action includes physical and mental action, emotional responses, and spiritual disciplines that lead to a desired outcome. If you take action from a place of fear or are constantly pushing to make something happen, you may be disappointed with your results.

Below is a simple guideline for those who are new to meditation. I highly recommend silent meditation which allows you to explore your thoughts. This meditation is not about quieting the mind—that takes greater practice. There is no goal here. Just sit and be. Take approximately fifteen minutes to do this exercise.

- Prepare the room by turning off the lights, phone, computer, and television.
- Light a candle.
- If you live with others, communicate your intentions so you will not be disturbed.
- Sit on a chair with feet flat on the floor.
- Relax your hands on the top of your thighs with palms facing up.
- Now close your eyes.
- Take three slow deep breaths in through your nose and release slowly again through your nose.
- Keep your focus on your breath.
- Observe your thoughts and sit in silence for fifteen minutes.
- If your thoughts become too overwhelming, say, "Thank you," to your thoughts and let them pass by. Return the focus to your breath.
- As you breathe, sit and listen to the silence that's around you.
- Congratulations! You're meditating and on the way to transforming your mind, soul, body, and life.

Meditation is known to reduce stress, enhance concentration, and heighten clarity in problem solving. For this reason, many business executives are tuning into the many benefits that meditation offers.

Leaders are known for making quick decisions. Enlightened leaders meditate first before making any decision. They let their Brilliant Self guide them in making the best possible choices that will serve everyone as they connect to their heart, values, and the principles that guide their lives. Whenever you are asked to make a decision, you can say, "I will meditate on the answer, and I will let you know my decision in 24 to 48 hours."

Today's Higher Idea: Practice the above meditation every evening to center yourself. You are the creator of your schedule, so it is important to take time for you and open up to your spirituality.

Higher Idea #65 Dissolving the Pain

This technique does take practice and it is not meant to replace your doctor's advice. I can only share my own experience of how I dissolved headaches, migraines, and back pain. I am happy to tell you that, to this day, I am pain free. You can learn to release the energy of pain through any of your seven main energy centers, also known as *chakras*. These energy centers are like universal doorways to health as they receive, process, and transmit universal energy. You actually have many energy centers in and around your physical body; however, for this exercise, let's just focus on one.

For example, if you have a headache, sit up straight and bring your full attention and awareness to the sixth chakra, your third eye area that is located in the middle of your forehead. Close your eyes and surrender to your imagination. First give the pain or toxic energy inside your head a form (it could be a cloud of energy or a black oily blob of goo; it doesn't matter what shape you give it.) Now visualize this heavy energy exiting through your third eye chakra or energy center. See the energy exit into a clear tube about six inches long. At the end of this tube, visualize a sphere of golden light. Allow all the dark energy in your head to pour out into the tube as if you were pouring water from a faucet and direct it into the sphere. Keep releasing energy until you see the color indigo, a deep blue, which is the natural color of this energy center. Now imagine that this sphere at the end of the tube is Source energy and is transmuting and dissolving the toxic energy. See the toxic energy disappear completely into the light.

Once you feel complete, and all the toxic energies from your head have been released, place your hands on your forehead and fill the inside of your head with loving energy. *Yes, you have healing hands!* Self-love heals everything. Most often, you will instantly feel an overwhelming sense of relief.

Today's Higher Idea: When releasing chaotic energy from your body, it is always important to acknowledge the gift or lesson. There is always a reason: for example, your pain may be reminding you to stop watching television that transmits negative or destructive images, or to drink more water.

Higher Idea #66 Play the Freedom Movie

Do you see a fearful future full of doom and gloom? Or do you see a future full of abundance, joy, and freedom? How you see your future determines the outcome. You determine your future by what you expect to see! You need to play the *freedom movie* in your mind to raise your vibration.

Your freedom movie is the movie you play in your mind that casts you in the leading role. This is a great way to train your subconscious mind and help you to expand your awareness of how you view yourself, your beloved, your family, and everyone else in your life. If you want others to show up differently, then you have to change the mental images you have of them. You are in charge of the script, the scenes, and the actors. You are the Divine star, director, and producer. Play the movie of your beautiful life. See yourself living the life you know you can. Visualize every detail, including *being* the man/woman you want to become. This exercise is great because you can release habitual thinking, feelings, and actions that no longer represent the amazing Divine being that is inside of you. You have the power to change the storyline at any time to create happy endings.

In order to take responsibility for what you have created in this world, you first need to acknowledge that you *are* a creator. You create the good, the bad, and the ugly with every thought vibration as well as the emotional charge attached to it. The good news is, if you are not happy with the life you have created so far, you have the power to change it. You have the power to create beauty, peace, and ultimate freedom.

Your subconscious mind communicates with imagery. It is your imagination that is the connecting link between the invisible and the visible, between the dream and the reality. If you want to train your mind and achieve your dreams, take a moment each day to visualize the YOU already living the life your heart desires. To create the best possible outcome in the next phase of your life, use your imagination and play the movie of *the life you intend to create,* with you as the star.

No matter what dream you visualize, these exercises are about *you,* not a fantasy version of you, but the *real* you. What I mean is: practice seeing yourself in your mind's eye just the way you are right now. This is a powerful practice in self-love and self-acceptance. To appreciate and love the Divine being you are right now will activate a deeper force within. If you are unable to see yourself in your mind's eye, that is okay. The more you practice, the clearer the image will become. Focus on the greatness that lives within you and your imaginary world will then pull these higher energies into your physical world. The more you visualize what you want to experience, the more you make the unknown *known*, which will empower you to disolve the fear of the unknown.

Creative imagery is more powerful when you add the element of *emotion*. When you construct an imagined reality in your mind and then create the *emotions* you will feel when you are there in that reality, those emotions will generate the necessary energy for your subconscious to believe it to be true. It will then go about making it so. As you visualize your future, bring in the energy of *joy*. Joy is the catalyst to all manifestation and will attract the circumstances and resources you need to make your vision a reality.

When you play your freedom movie, remember to remain focused on creating *your* life. You are not here to influence anyone else's journey without permission. So, when you visualize, focus only on yourself, as much as possible. If you bring others into your creative dreaming, only see the good. For example, if you are driving home from work and think your spouse/partner will be miserable or unhappy when you get there, then that is what you will experience. Instead, visualize your beloved happy. See yourself giving them a hug and letting them know you are happy to see them. Only project out thoughts and images you want to experience. When you create destructive images, others will feel them energetically in their physical world. We are all connected, so be mindful.

It is not a good idea to stay in dreamland for hours because you do have a life to live. Your present moment requires your full attention, so only spend thirty minutes per day inviting and training your subconscious mind to live in freedom. The best time to train your subconscious mind with higher thoughts, words, and images is prior to falling asleep.

Whenever you have moments where you're losing sight of your dream, play the *freedom movie* in your mind. See and feel yourself living the life you want to live. Visualize yourself being successful because you found a solution to a problem. See yourself uplifting all souls in some way. See yourself as a bestselling author because you have a powerful story of inspiration to share. Consciously creating mental images and feeling yourself there allows you to go beyond your present circumstance.

You may have had moments where you asked the universe, "What the heck is going on?" Welcome to the club. Do not compare your life to anyone else's. Trust that life is working for you behind the scenes. If you are in doubt, have lost your faith, or feel like you are doing all the inner work and still nothing is happening; keep going! Be patient. Recommit to the vision that your heart seeks to experience.

Today's Higher Idea: Play your freedom movie and *embrace* your Joyful Self, your Abundant Self, your Fun Self, and your Healthy Self who are here to empower you in living the life you are here to live.

Higher Idea #67 Trust Your Intuition

Has your Intuitive Self become a Forgotten Angel? Your Intuitive Self is the voice of inner knowing. Intuition enables you to define what vibration you are presently in. Your intuition is the voice within that offers you the biggest rewards in life—if you choose to listen. Your intuition embodies your divinity, or what some refer to as your spirit guides and teachers. Your Intuitive Self is with you now, waiting patiently to assist you in living your Divine purpose, which is the reason why you came to this planet in the first place. The *Divine Mind Conversation* (Higher Idea #79) offers a simple way of connecting to your Intuitive Self and the many Forgotten Angels alive inside of you. You can ask your Intuitive or Brilliant Self to give you guidance at any time.

Although the mind is wondrous, the spiritual dimension connects you to the principles you live by. Connecting to your intuition will give you the courage to explore the dark caverns of your mind, those places you were once afraid of. Knowing that you have an inner power that is ready to assist you can bring about a sense of relief and greater trust in your life process. You learn to make the unknown known by expanding your awareness and connecting to your Intuitive Self, which will guide you through uncertainty.

Florence Scovel Shinn wrote in her book, *The Wisdom of Florence Scovel Shinn*, "prayer is telephoning to God and intuition is God telephoning to you. Many people have a busy wire when God telephones and they don't get the message. Your wire is busy when you are discouraged, angry, or resentful. Your negative emotions can drown out the voice of intuition."

Today's Higher Idea: Tap your third eye three times and ask your Intuitive Self to help you see more. Now repeat, "I do not have an answer to my problem. I have no idea what to do. I have no idea how I will manifest _____. I am letting go of knowing how it will happen." Take a deep breath. Now you have allowed your ego to get out of your way and opened the door to your Divine Mind, your True Self, who will bring you the answer or solution you seek.

Higher Idea #68 Imagine the Possibilities of Wealth

As a struggling entrepreneur, I've had many moments when I've experienced the roller-coaster of feast or famine. With no money in my bank account and unable to pay my rent, I often thought I was crazy for taking this journey, because even though my soul was guiding me to experience all that I was, *love* was not paying the bills. In the moments when I just wanted to pack it all in, my Brilliant Self would remind me, "*Wealth is your natural state. Abundance is your natural state. Keep going!*"

Money offers physical freedom—the freedom to experience the material world and the pleasures of life. Unfortunately, many who are wealthy have material possessions, yet they live very stressful, unhappy lives, and often drown in the drug and alcohol culture. Rich men/women experience depression and loneliness just like anyone else. What I am suggesting is for you to become rich and wealthy on the inside first by connecting with your Forgotten Angels. Then you will be better equipped to handle the higher vibrations of unlimited wealth.

For most of my life, I lived in default, allowing my Fallen Angels to control my life. Talk about a roller-coaster ride! At times, I couldn't understand why I was in the circumstance I was in or why clients were not calling, no matter how much action I took. There were many times I was taken to my knees and had to rely on the kindness of others. I had connected to my Wealthy Self, my Abundant Self, and my Worthy Self. I felt clear and open to these higher vibrations, yet I was not experiencing the sustainable financial wealth I knew I was meant to enjoy. Again, my Brilliant Self would show me an image of my stepfather, smiling and waving at me. Ahh, yes! The message was loud and clear (See Higher Idea #74). Everything was happening for a reason, even if I did not see it in the moment.

My years of experience have taught me that wealth is not about money. Wealth reflects your emotional and mental state. Just as lack is a state of mind, wealth is also a state of mind. We are either in poverty consciousness (fear frequency) or wealth consciousness (*Freedom Frequency*). Many of us have been conditioned to believe we do not deserve abundance. Many of us think that if we *have* nothing, then we *are* nothing. On the other end of the spectrum, many of us may feel that the more material things we have, the more complete we are.

When you are vibrating in the Freedom Frequency, you have a wealth of opportunities available to you. You recognize the wealth of friendship, the wealth of family, and the wealth of love in your life. You also have a wealth of creative expression to share with the world.

If you are stuck in the *fear of losing it all* or the *fear of losing control,* you will stop the flow of wealth. Only when you stop beating yourself up and disapproving of yourself can you shift your vibration and attract more abundance. If you have attachments to your possessions, life will teach you to become unattached. We can enjoy all the material things created in the world so long as they do not possess us. Materialism is not meant to control you.

If there is a part of you that believes in *lack,* it is because you are allowing your Lack self (the ego) to control you like a puppet on a string. Your Lack self will have you believe you are worthless and that you will always have *nothing.* It is time to face your Lack self and take your power back. The Lack self is a Fallen Angel that holds the seed of all lack within you. The more you are afraid of this self or ignore this aspect of you, the more power this *self* has over you. The Lack self only represents one cherry in your Divine cherry pie, and when you have the courage to face this *self* and say, "I will no longer let you control me. I now take my power back!" your life will open up.

As you communicate with your Lack self, you will discover that this *self* was really only lacking *love* from you. That is all any of your Fallen Angels want. As you acknowledge, forgive, and learn how to love this part of you, the negative energetic charge will release. You will see your Lack self transform and your Abundant Self will appear. This Forgotten Angel is now remembered, and as you embody these higher vibrations, you align yourself with the infinite supply of abundance, which brings the Divine beings, resources, and opportunities you require to move forward in your life.

If you do not have the physical freedom to explore externally, then you are being called to explore yourself internally and cultivate the energy of abundance from within. As you transform your internal world and implant new empowering beliefs about yourself, you will release your resistance to shining your light into the external world. The lack of money will also teach you powerful lessons in humility and gratitude, so you remain humble and grateful no matter what sphere of reality you are living in.

Many fears begin to surface when the possibility of losing everything is close at hand, such as fear of losing control, fear of loss, fear of pain, fear of the unknown, or fear of what others may think. However, this is good because now you can release these illusions that have kept you living small. Here, in these fears, is where you need to stay present with the energy of it and just breathe through it. Remember, your ego will resist the higher idea of you connecting to your I AM Presence, which is already abundant.

Many of us attempt to create heaven by surrounding themselves with beautiful things. However, if hell still exists in your mind, you will be living a game you cannot win. Take the time to connect with your Forgotten Angels and integrate with them so you can empower yourself from the inside out.

Today's Higher Idea: Connect to your Wealthy and/or Abundant Self by imagining that you just won the lottery. It is not about the money. It is the feeling that nothing is missing, and you no longer want for anything. Cultivate this energy of abundance and you create a new world for you, your family, and us all. Say to yourself, "I AM wealth. There is an infinite supply, and I am connected to this infinite supply."

Higher Idea #69 Creativity Links You to Abundance

You are here to create! Remember, dreamers and visionaries built this world. Everything that was ever invented, from the chair you're sitting on to the clothes you're wearing, came through the world of imagination. The world of imagination is very real, and the more you understand how it works, the more ability you have to bring new ideas into this physical world to be experienced.

The material world and the spiritual world are not separate— they are one. If you are afraid of one world, you are also afraid of the other. Explore both worlds and discover the beauty in all creation. We are here to craft and share our creations with the world. Money moves the creation process into the material world.

Moving into a higher consciousness of infinite possibilities takes time, so be patient and remember to enjoy your present moment. For example, if you do not appreciate the job you have or you are unhappy in your relationship, flip the idea and view it as your training ground for bigger things to come. Learn the lessons placed before you and always give the best of yourself. This practice will demonstrate that you have a learning attitude about life. You will know intuitively if and when it is time to move on.

While sitting in meditation, all my programs, workshops, games, and books were revealed. There is an infinite supply of ideas just waiting to be created and experienced here on earth. Wealth is given to those who create solutions to the world's problems. You have access to an infinite number of creative ideas just waiting to be birthed through you.

Learn to enjoy the creative process of your life. If you *trust* that all your creations are Divinely inspired, then you no longer need to stress out about how or when you are going to accomplish something.

Today's Higher Idea: If you have created a product or service, let go of the lower idea that you're somehow going to miss out on your piece of the pie or share of the market. This is fear-based thinking. You live in an abundant universe and there is plenty for all. The more you focus on creating value for others and living in gratitude, the more you draw abundance to you. Universal Intelligence will naturally supply you with the right customers or clients who are seeking your products or services.

Higher Idea #70 See the Bigger Picture

If you're uncomfortable with the concept of God, then you are uncomfortable with your own Divinity. When we believe God is just "out there" or a man with a beard in the sky, we immediately create separation. We have made a division between our outer and inner worlds. Some religious followers worship deities outside of themselves, ignoring the internal Source, *the Divine light* within us all.

We have many names for God, such as: Love, Higher Power, Allah, Universal Intelligence, Divine Mind, Source, Creator, and *Goddess*. The Creator is a concept that exists in virtually every culture in some way. It's important to remember that our Creator is not racist or prejudiced. It is love, abundance, and truth. The Divine Mind is the source of all things. However, when we only see the Creator as *out there*, we may see ourselves as "lesser than" or "just human." It's time to focus on the internal God or Goddess, the Divine Creator within all things and within every one of us.

We often forget that the essence of the Creator moves through us. A higher idea is to remember that *the God vibration can penetrate your skin.*

We'll never truly know who we are if all we do is idolize what's outside of ourselves. What if you stopped looking up at the heavens and instead looked within? The moment we let go of a particular image of the Creator, we become capable of shifting focus and seeing God as an omnipresent energy penetrating and infusing all things. In this way, we're no longer separate from Life. We know we are connected to All That Is. See life from a higher perspective and allow the bigger picture to unfold.

Today's Higher Idea: What if you visualized God, the Source of all things within all things, and knew that every being is a unique expression of the Creator, of Universal Intelligence? How differently would you view others? How differently would you see yourself?

Chapter Seven
Integration of Your Divine Mind

Within you is a powerful field of higher intelligence, known as your Divine Mind. Your Divine Mind is the Observer of the many selves that make up the totality of you. When you enter this unified field of consciousness, you are liberated from the suffering caused by the creations manufactured by the fear-based mind, the *ego,* and the separation of self.

Each Higher Idea written in this book offers a path to your Divine Mind—an enlightened state of mind where you see yourself as whole and complete. As you integrate all of these higher ideas into your life, you will begin to experience a quantum leap in how you feel inside. You will be vibrating at a higher frequency, allowing your Brilliant Self, the highest version of you, to integrate into your physical body.

As you align with your Divine Mind, your vibration expands with incredible force, and everyone is touched by it. Imagination becomes reality and life is unlimited. You discover the art of living. You no longer need to conform to others' ideals. You are no longer focused on self-fulfillment; you are focused on creating value for the greater good. You have a learning attitude and are open to infinite possibilities. You're in the realm of freedom, doing what you love and sharing it with others.

Integration of your Divine Mind takes you beyond the old stories of illness, wrongness, faults, and projections of the fear-based mind. You now remember you are divinely perfect in every moment as you are an expression of All That Is, the Source of all things manifested.

Higher Idea #71 Step Out of the Spiritual Closet

Are you afraid of what others may think of your spiritual beliefs? Spirituality is not a religion and it's not "New Age." Spirituality is a way of life and is the alignment with Source energy. Spirituality is the devotion to integrating mind and heart, a journey toward truth.

Many of us have lived in a spiritual closet because we're afraid of being criticized or condemned for our truths. This fear changes as we allow ourselves to listen fully and accept others for who they are, even if their spiritual beliefs are not our own. The less you criticize or condemn others for their beliefs, the less you will experience criticism in your own life.

There are times when you play the role of a teacher, and other times when you play the role of a student. Playing the role of a spiritual guide or teacher requires the skills to explain what you mean with calmness and integrity. Playing the role of a student gives you the space to learn something new that may be very beneficial in the development of your mind and soul. To become a student of life means having an open heart and mind, as well as a learning attitude. As you devote yourself to the path of higher values, you'll set standards that others will want to follow.

Many eastern philosophies advocate that we are here to spiral up from one plane of consciousness to another. When you are vibrating at a higher frequency, you are often invisible to others who are functioning in lower vibratory fields, like the *frequency of fear*. The only ones you will attract are those who are ready and willing to learn through you, those who are ready to live in the light of self-awareness.

By acknowledging your Divine presence, you become a magnet in the light and no longer need to force or push anything to manifest in your life. Everything begins to unfold naturally and in connection with your soul's purpose.

Today's Higher Idea: Have friends over for dinner and have everyone share one thing about her or his spiritual journey that has made a profound difference in her or his life.

Higher Idea #72 Connect to Your Brilliant Self

What would your response be if someone asked you, "What motivates you to do the things you do or say the things you say?" Many respond to this question with the statement, "I don't know. I just do what I do." We tend to go through life on autopilot, buying this, doing that, saying this, and at times being completely unaware of the motivating factors behind our words or actions.

Remember, a powerful universal force flows through you. If you acknowledge this Divine intelligence, you'll activate the opening of spiritual channels that allow you to communicate and receive higher wisdom.

You are here to recognize the Divine power that spirals through you. The light of your soul remains hidden until you revive it with your conscious mind. Only then will your soul come back to you and lead you out of the fear frequency into the light of truth—the truth of who you are.

Higher worlds of love are obtained through disciplining the mind, emotional integrity, and a strong spiritual connection. Powerful tools for opening the heart and connecting you to the spiritual dimension are:

- Meditation – connects you to your feeling center.
- Deep Breathing – connects you to life force energy.
- Trusting Your Intuition – connects you to your inner wisdom.
- Healthy Imagination – connects you to your creativity.

You also connect to the spiritual dimension through empowering others. Lifting others up will bring you joy and a greater sense of belonging in the world. It's important to remember to assist only those who are ready to see and experience the truth; otherwise, you'll exhaust yourself by trying to force others to see or feel what they may not be ready to grasp.

The spiritual energy that flows through you will also empower you to solve every problem, no matter how big. Connecting to Universal intelligence is achieved by raising your consciousness. Consciousness refers to the level of awareness of who you are, the life you have created, and the reality you live in.

Your journey on earth becomes less complicated, stressful, and chaotic when you make every effort to connect with your Forgotten Angels. The more you lighten up your mind and physical body (the temple of your soul), the more you see that the path you are on is divinely perfect. When you are connected to your Divine Intelligence, your Brilliant Self, you no longer need to fear for your safety. You will always be guided to the right place at the right time.

Today's Higher Idea: Ask yourself, "Does my Fearful self control my mind or does my Brilliant Self guide me?" A powerful exercise is to visualize the knowledge of the Universe as liquid golden light entering the top of your head, filling your brain, and spiralling down into every cell of your body. With every breath, you ask your cells to revive and activate your soul's blueprint.

Higher Idea #73 Be of Service to Others

Being of service is about giving without any expectation of receiving something in return. This is unconditional *giving,* and at the same time, there is no giving when you are in the Freedom Frequency. You are simply flowing universal energy to the one who is before you. You are aware of what needs to be done and you offer your energy from a place of ease and grace. Selfless service is about honouring the Divine presence in each and every being.

Being of service is a wonderful spiritual practice. Here you can identify whether you are giving from a place of divine essence, or giving because the ego wants to be recognized. If you are giving from the place of "Look at how good I am," then this is giving from the *ego.* Selfless service is from the heart and needs no acknowledgement.

You can be of service to your beloved, your family, to a group, community, or cause. Being of service involves connecting to what matters most to you. A conscious entrepreneur creates a business to help solve a problem and to be of service to the world. We are all here to make a difference and harmoniously collaborate.

In the Freedom Frequency, you no longer place yourself above others and you no longer see others on a pedestal. Instead of thinking, "What's in it for me?", your *focus* is on how you can make a difference and add value to the lives of others.

Being in a high vibration of health and well-being is important if you want to serve others in the best way possible. Being of service should not cost you more than you can afford financially, physically, spiritually, or emotionally.

Remember, no one can take advantage of you unless you let them. True happiness and ultimate freedom are measured by how much you give, not by what you receive. When you give from the heart, you expand your capacity to receive more joy and fulfillment in your life.

Today's Higher Idea: Become aware of the self within that asks, "What is in it for me?" Let this inner Fallen Angel know this attitude is no longer acceptable and you are now reframing your question to, "What can I do to make a positive difference in someone's life today?"

Higher Idea #74 Listen to Your Higher Self

I have a true story I want to share with you. I love travelling, so a few years ago I planned a road trip to Arizona with a man I was living with at the time. I had been to Arizona a few years earlier with a girlfriend and had fallen in love with the beauty of the desert.

As I was sitting at my computer planning our trip, I heard a voice in my head that said, "Take your mom and John (stepdad) on the trip." I ignored the voice at first because I wanted to make this a romantic road trip with my guy. My Higher Self was persistent and kept repeating the words, "Take your mom and John on the trip," until I took action and called my mom. I asked her whether she and John wanted to travel with us to Arizona. Delighted with the idea, they said, "Yes."

Within a few weeks, we were off on our two-week road trip from Calgary to Phoenix. My mom and John were the perfect travel companions, and even though they were both seniors, they acted like excited children, laughing and enjoying every moment. They explored the Grand Canyon and in Sedona, to celebrate my mom's seventy-second birthday, they took their first ever helicopter tour. But what was truly amazing was that there was not one argument between the four of us the entire trip.

About six months later, my Higher Self said the same words again; "Take your mom and John on a trip." Well, this time I hadn't been planning on going anywhere but I remembered that my mom and

John had purchased a time-share. However, I again ignored the voice because I was busy marketing and creating my website for my coaching business and did not feel I had the time to go anywhere. Or so I thought.

Finally, listening to my persistent Higher Self, I called my mom and asked whether they wanted to go on another trip. Well, my mom immediately said that she had an aunt and a cousin in Pasadena who she would love to see. I love empowering others and making their dreams come true, so I booked a flight, and within a week, my mom, John, and I were flying to Los Angeles for a week's holiday.

It was on this trip that I discovered many things about my stepdad, John. I found out that he had never worn shorts or running shoes! I was totally amazed, but then knowing him, I quickly understood. He was an eighty-year-old Scottish gentleman who always dressed sharply. To our surprise, he actually bought himself a pair of walking shorts and running shoes. He laughed when he saw his legs and joked about how white they were.

Driving down the coast, I was drawn to pull over into a beachside parking lot. I suggested to my mom and John that we go for a walk along the beach. We all took our shoes off, walked across the sand, and walked in the water.

As I took pictures of Mom and John laughing like children, I realized my stepdad had tears in his eyes. When I asked him if he was okay, he said, "I'm in my eighty years, and I have never felt the ocean on my toes before."

We had many *firsts* on that trip, and I was so glad, once again, to have followed through with the wisdom of my Higher Self.

Two months later, guess what? The voice, again! Yes, I was hearing the same words: *"Take your parents on a trip."* This time I didn't hesitate to listen. I felt drawn to invite my whole family, which included my boyfriend, my brother Dwayne, my mom and John, as well as my dad and my stepmom. And yes, both sets of parents are great friends, which is an amazing story in itself.

I organized and planned a four-day trip for all seven of us to fly to New York City to experience the Big Apple together. My brother Dwayne and I had been to New York several times, attending tradeshows over the years, but this was a first for everyone else. We laughed, cried, and deepened our connections over a dinner harbour tour, awed by the architecture and amazing sights of Manhattan.

Again, two months later, I was sitting at my computer writing when once more my Higher Self said, "Take your parents on a trip." It sounded a little crazy, but I had learned to listen even if I did not know the reason in that moment.

So, I called my mom and John and asked whether they wanted to travel to California and spend her seventy-third birthday in Santa Barbara. They immediately said, "Yes," so the three of us were off for another adventure. I chauffeured them up the coast to a beautiful resort where we wined and dined, laughed till we cried, relaxed, and rejuvenated. I was amazed with the transformation that had taken place within my stepdad over the past year because I had known him to have quite a temper. He was embracing his sense of humour and he had us laughing for hours.

A week after arriving home, my mom called to ask me whether we could go to Hawaii on our next trip. I love Hawaii, so I was thrilled with their choice of a tropical destination. When I hung up the phone, I sat for a moment and realized I did not have the same sense of urgency as I had experienced when planning previous trips. I did not hear the words I had become so used to hearing from my Higher Self. Within a month I discovered why. My stepfather was diagnosed with leukemia, and within a week, he passed away.

I share this incredible experience with you to encourage you to always listen to your voice of intuition, even if it doesn't seem to make sense at the time. Your Higher Self always knows what is best for you and others, and if you listen, you are sure to be guided on an amazing adventure.

I am so grateful that I took the time to listen. I got to see and experience, in a completely different way, a man I had known for many years. These trips were a blessing for all of us and I have memories I will always cherish. Just hours before he passed away, my stepdad took my hand, tears in both our eyes, and he said, *"Karen, thank you for giving me the best year of my life."*

Six months later, I took my mom to Maui, Hawaii and we were given many gifts from spirit, one which was whale watching and to our amazement 5 whales, one after another, gave us a full breach show. The tour guide said that he'd never seen anything like it in all the years he had been out in the boat.

Today's Higher Idea: Stay open to opportunities even when you "think" you do not have time or money. Your Higher Self can see the future and the enfoldment of events far clearer than you ever could. Trust that when you are asked to assist, it is the Universe calling.

Higher Idea #75 You Live in an Abundant Universe

Since money is man-made, why is it that we seem to need, crave, and do almost anything to have this product? Why are we judged if we do not have this product (materialism)? If we have no money in our bank accounts, why is it we are deemed *failures*? Why do we link money to our self-worth?

These are powerful questions, and now more than ever, we are beginning to realize that self-worth has nothing to do with what we have in our bank accounts or in achievements. If the financial system crashed, would that mean we were all worthless? No. Self-worth is realized when you are connected to the true source of abundance. The true source of abundance is not money, your employer, or your clients or customers. The true source of abundance is God, your I AM presence, the Source, the Universe, Creator, or whatever name you give this Infinite Intelligence. The God Vibration flows through every human being and throughout all of life, and it is the source of all wealth, health, wisdom, love, joy, prosperity, creativity, abundance, and miracles.

There is an infinite supply of resources and opportunities available for every one of us. Yes, you can actually have what you want, knowing that no one will be deprived of getting what they want. This is how abundant our universe is. If you listen to your inner Fallen Angels that say, "I am not worthy; I do not deserve more—there isn't enough" or "I will go last to make sure everyone gets what they want," then these beliefs will disconnect you from the Source and separate you from the infinite supply of abundance.

You may have wondered, "If this is an abundant universe, then why are so many suffering in poverty and little ones dying of hunger?" This question is not easily answered. However, we do not know the journey of each soul and the life lessons it is to experience.

There are many powerful souls who have made a choice to come to this realm and live for a short time, or in poverty, or playing out a victim role so others can learn valuable life lessons through them, such as compassion, love, and selfless service. I was once on welfare, but now I am an author, and one of the co-founders of Life Force Canada. Who knew?

The best advice I can offer is to send others your blessings and love and then bring the focus back on you. Change your life first so you can be the example of what is possible.

If your vibration resonates in fear, you will block yourself from receiving the abundance that is only a frequency away. Spiralling up and out of the world of lack or a poverty consciousness involves mental, emotional, and spiritual discipline and devotion. As you expand and create wealth within your mind and trust that there is more than enough for everyone, you will begin to experience a world that is full of resources, opportunities, love, support, food, and money. It is your wealth frequency and living above the line that will draw these things into your life.

As I mentioned in Higher Idea #69, it is your creativity, the divine gift within, that you are here to share with the world. When you are connected to Infinite Source, you will be guided to meet the Divine beings who are seeking what you offer.

Trust that you are always provided with exactly what you need at the right time. The more you tune into the Freedom Frequency, the more you tune into an abundant life. All that is required is remembering the truth—that you are worthy and are here on this planet to enjoy the best life has to offer.

Today's Higher Idea: Ask and you shall receive. Focus on how you would feel if you had everything you wanted. Say to yourself, "I live in an abundant universe and there is plenty for all of us."

Higher Idea #76 We Are All One

Many of us have become divided in our thoughts, creating separation or *duality* in our daily life experiences. Now we can truly recognize that the fear frequency isn't separate from the Freedom Frequency. The frequencies are just at opposite ends of the spectrum, like two sides of a coin. We cannot have freedom unless we have experienced its opposite. Once we thoroughly understand fear and embrace the gift, we see that the only thing left is the truth of our existence. Nothing is separate; we are all mirrors of each other expressing our own unique and creative selves.

This book focuses on the duality of fear and freedom, the dark and the light, to show you how divided you may have become within your own mind. This division is only for the sake of learning and identifying the energies that are alive inside of you. Once you come to terms with what fear is—*the ultimate illusion*—it transforms, and all that remains is the truth that only *love* is real.

You recognize that all chaos, tragedy, trauma, change, or destruction bring the necessary adjustments required to manifest higher energy vibrations in the Freedom Frequency of life.

We have chosen to see fear and freedom as being in two different places. We have chosen to see our emotions and our life as good or bad, positive or negative, and right or wrong. The polarity of third dimensional living is dissolving as we spiral up into higher dimensions and remember that at the core of all existence is LOVE, *enlightened love*. Enlightened love is the Divine glue that unifies everything.

When you let go of duality *within*—the good and bad perspectives—and consciously choose to see only the unity and perfection of All That Is, your life harmonizes.

When we begin to believe that we have learned everything we can from the world of pain and suffering, which is ultimately the separation of our own Divine nature, we will spiral up out of fear-based living. We have ignored, forgotten, resisted, and feared who we are long enough. We are coming *alive* and remembering that we have collectively created this earthly experience and all its contrasts. We're all brothers and sisters on an earthly journey, and it's time to come home to ourselves. It's time for all of us to breathe in unity and see the Divine plan in all its magnificence.

As we integrate the divine masculine and divine feminine energies that flow through us, we see heaven within our own minds which is then reflected out into our experience. As we send love to all the creatures that inhabit this beautiful planet, we embrace global love. We are *love* and we will experience this divine truth the more we choose to appreciate and respect the Earth, dissolve the idea of winners or losers, know that we are all gifted Divine beings, release our fear of one another, integrate darkness into light, and choose to uplift everyone around us.

The *Freedom Frequency* is embodying your Divine nature. When you have internal freedom, you experience external freedom. Spirit is calling you to explore your inner worlds and acknowledge your Fallen and Forgotten Angels so you can integrate and become ONE, the Remembered Angel.

You no longer need to learn from fear. You are complete. You are now remembering who you are and letting go of all you are *not,* so you may emerge with the highest expression of who you are. Now, together, we create heaven on earth.

Today's Higher Idea: Embrace your divinity by sending loving thought vibrations out to all the beings of earth.

Higher Idea #77 See the Divine Order in Your Life

At the core of all things, at their vibratory level, is absolute perfect order. This means that at the core of who you are is *Divine Intelligence*.

Your power is in the present moment. Only when you are present can you see the Divine order of life. Even when things appear at their worst, there is Divine order. For example, when doors of opportunity and abundance close, it is usually a sign that you are being called to go within and shift your internal world. Once *thought adjustments* are made and you are in Divine alignment, the supply of abundance will reopen its doors. Order and flow are always restored.

When you're vibrating in the Freedom Frequency, you will never experience loneliness because you remember that you are not alone. You may experience aloneness, which is very different than feeling lonely. In the reality of this freedom, you no longer have a need to escape circumstances. You make the choice to experience the moment fully, and to embrace the richness of it.

When you recognize the Divine order of life, you trust that you are in the right place at the right time and engaged in exactly what you're meant to be doing at that moment. Trust that when the money runs out, more money will appear. Or when one project fails, another project will materialize. Or when an opportunity is missed, another door will open. As you flow in thoughts of abundance, life flows along with you.

Today's Higher Idea: How will you spark your divinity today?

Higher Idea #78 Breathe in the Light

Shining your light and your love into the world involves opening your heart and giving of yourself. Some of us mistakenly believe that if we *give,* we won't have. It's not about being a martyr and forgetting about your own needs. The kind of giving I'm referring to is empowering others to help make their dreams come true, whether it's giving advice, energy, direction, financial assistance, or, most importantly, our time. An attitude of self-gratification is transformed when we consider others and show them we truly care.

Light is love! When you are no longer afraid of your light, then you are living on purpose which is to be the *light* that you are, the *love* that you are, and share your vibration with the world. Some may not understand or accept the journey you're on. You may be laughed at, ignored, gossiped about, yelled at, and/or told to stop dreaming foolish dreams and to get a real job. Some may even stop loving you.

On the path to living above the line, you'll have some who may tell you that you'll never make it. Even some of your friends may not believe in you. Will any of this stop you? Remember, when you are connected to your soul's mission, you will ignore those who seek to instill fear and doubt. When you live with purpose you will only listen to those who inspire and give encouragement. Keep refining, enhancing, and expressing your vision.

If the satellites in the sky focused on you, they would see a light so bright that those viewing the images would think it was a small city.

You have a star inside of you just waiting for the moment to shine brightly for all to see.

A star's journey is never an overnight success. Whether you want to perform for others or create products or services that uplift us all, it's up to you. Just live with an open heart and your life will be prosperous. Do you remember the movie, *Pay It Forward?* That's one of my favourite movies because I believe if we have the courage to spread our light, we open ourselves up to a new way of living and being.

Today's Higher Idea: Shine your light and your love on everyone you meet from this day forward.

Higher Idea #79 Divine Mind Conversations

Many of us have a difficult time approaching issues or problems in our relationships or in our businesses because of our fear of conflict. We have developed the belief that, "If I talk about this issue, I will become disappointed, I will disappoint others, or I will be criticized." Unresolved issues eventually magnify over time causing resentment, blame, and disconnection.

The *Divine Mind Conversation* was designed to transform the relationship you have with yourself so you can transform the relationships you have with others. It is a powerful tool you can use to face issues in your life without having to face anyone directly. This process shifts the negative energetic charge you have toward others and yourself, and prepares you for healthy emotional expression. This will help you approach anyone, talk about anything, and, at the same time, keep your vibration above the line.

So how does it work? As I mentioned earlier, it is best to have a facilitator guide you through the first time, so you are completely aware of the steps involved. You are working with a very intelligent source that lives inside of you—it must be contained and approached with the deepest of respect. Skipping steps will not give you the desired results. If steps are taken with guidance, the end result is a direct experience of enlightenment (*lightening up*).

The *Divine Mind Conversation* was shown to me in meditation many years ago and it has assisted me in discovering deeper parts of myself that I did not know existed. If it was true that my invisible worlds—my mental, emotional, and spiritual dimensions—created my physical experience, I knew that if I were to transform my life, I had to find a way to communicate with these invisible aspects of myself.

The *Divine Mind Conversation* is a seven-step process that combines creative imagery and self-hypnosis. The complete experience is realized through your imagination. Here, you become consciously aware of the sensations in your body that either react or respond to images appearing in your mind. Your imagination offers you insight (*inner sight*) to see beyond your five senses. If you are worried that you will have a hard time seeing or conjuring images within your mind because you haven't been able to in the past, that is okay. Magic seems to happen as the pineal gland activates, giving you the ability to see full color pictures, even if you have never been able to before.

The *Divine Mind Conversation* will empower you to see yourself from many different angles of reflection. You will know the process is working when the images you are creating cause tears to surface or tingles to arise in your body. You may feel uncomfortable as truth emerges. Then a rush of energy bursts through, offering relief, and potentially freedom, as you now accept and see yourself from a completely new perspective. These are all signs that the process is shifting your internal world and releasing negative energy that no longer serves you.

Below is a very brief summary of the seven steps involved.

Step One: Enter your Divine Mind. The *Divine Mind Conversation* begins with imagining a mansion in your Divine Mind, the unified field of consciousness. You then open the door and enter into a white room known as the Purification Room. This space is infused with the highest vibration, *enlightened love*. Here, any and all dark and negative thoughts, ideas, or forces that create separation are dissolved and transmuted. In this room there is a table and three chairs. Two chairs are at one end of the table for you and your Brilliant Self (the highest version of who you are) and a third chair us at the other end of the table.

Step Two: Meet Your Fallen Angel. Now bring forth *one* inner Fallen Angel that is causing you the most problems in your life and have that Fallen Angel sit across from you. Sometimes it is easier to begin with visualizing someone in your life with whom you have a lot of unresolved anger. If you have a negative association with any family member, friend, or co-worker, then they could represent a Fallen Angel in your mind.

Step Three: Express All Incomplete Communication. It is here that you have an opportunity to transform your emotional pain by directing and expressing all the unspoken communication and the truth of how you feel to the Fallen Angel that sits before you. Give yourself permission to vent with your inner voice instead of your outer voice, which releases all the pent-up negative energy that has been suppressed. Whatever you express within the inner realm of your Divine Mind, such as anger, rage, hate, or sadness, is instantly transmuted and dissolved into the light without any karmic effect occurring in your physical reality. Do not hold back any emotion. Stay here until the energy in your body has neutralized or you feel relieved, lighter, or liberated. Take a deep breath!

Step Four: Become the Observer. Now it is your turn to listen and feel the power of vulnerability by giving your Fallen Angel a voice and listening to every word. Yes, that Fallen Angel will express words you have been afraid to hear in your outer life. Some words may shock you. Just breathe deeply and slowly. Learning to listen and observe without taking it personally is the practice. As you observe, you will begin to see that it is only your inner Fallen Angels who hold the seeds of anger, frustration, hate, stress, and so on. Once you recognize and completely understand that the anger, stress, frustration, or any other perceived negative emotion you experience does not come from any external source, you are *enlightened*. The negative emotions or states only come from your mind, from the inner intelligence of a Fallen Angel. Listen with compassion and have a learning attitude. Breathe deeply!

Step Five: Forgive Your Fallen Angels. You begin to shift your vibration when you no longer believe that what your Fallen Angels are saying is true. It is their story, and you are only here to acknowledge and not judge what they say as wrong or right, good or bad. If you attempt to kick out, throw out, or banish a Fallen Angel, its energy will strengthen. It is your love and forgiveness that will dissolve the negative energetic charge associated with each Fallen Angel. Now you can say within your mind, "Thank you for meeting me here. I am so sorry it took so long for me to see you, hear you, and acknowledge you. Please forgive me."

Step Six: Be Open to Receiving the Gift. Every inner self has a divine message for you that can assist you in moving forward. Once the energy projected from your Fallen Angel has neutralized, you can let them know the truth that they are loved and accepted by you. Ask the inner Fallen Angel before you, "What message do you have for me? What is it you need from me?" Now listen. Take a deep breath. Can you commit honouring their request? Remember, their request must serve your highest good.

Step Seven: Walk into the Light of Integration. Once you have received the message, say, "Thank you," and then visualize both of you walking through a door and leaving the room of your Divine Mind. You are now in a beautiful garden standing in the sunlight, the light of integration, the light of knowing you have the power to transform darkness into light. Take three deep-belly breaths. And so it is.

Higher Idea #80 You Are the Remembered Angel

The *Divine Mind Conversations* will show you how to stop projecting your negative emotions outwardly toward others and to *turn around* and go within to face your Fallen Angels in the white room of your Divine Mind.

The *Divine Mind Conversation* is a powerful tool to bring forth all your inner Forgotten Angels who will assist you in vibrating at a higher frequency. Once you acknowledge each Forgotten Angel, such as your Passionate Self, your Happy Self, your Grateful Self, your Joyful Self, your Wealthy Self, your Wise Self, your Healthy Self and so on, they transform into Remembered Angels. These positive or higher qualities live inside you, and it is up to you to integrate all these higher vibrations so you can spiral up and live above the line.

Yes, you have the power to transform and release all negative emotions and limited beliefs. Through the process of using your imagination and your emotions to *feel* everything, you release your Fallen Angels into the light and integrate all your Forgotten Angels that offer the riches of life.

Over time as you continue this practice, you will know you are complete when all the voices that hold a negative energetic charge have left the building, the mansion of your Divine Mind. When all voices have become unified, you will be standing with one voice, the voice of your Brilliant Self.

You are meant to live above the line in the frequency of love, *enlightened love*. You are not your fear. You are not your beliefs. You are not your emotions. You are not your body. You are remembering that all the angels that live inside you are to be integrated. Each angel symbolizes an *angle* of light that you are here to reflect. You are here to integrate each one until you are left with only ONE angel—YOU!

You are the ONE we have been waiting for.

The REMEMBERED Angel!

Whole and complete.

Here to create heaven on earth.

From the Author

There comes a moment in everyone's life when all the pieces of the puzzle join together, and the lines vanish. The life picture you once dreamt about is clear and unfolding before you. Finally! You realize all the effort you've put into disciplining your emotional, mental, spiritual, and physical dimensions, as well as everything in between, was well worth it. It's as if all the planets and stars have aligned and now your dreams have become reality.

The most important question I want you to ask yourself and remember is: *Where are you vibrating—fear or freedom?* Awareness of your energetic vibration is the key to living above the line. Remember, your thoughts and emotions are constantly sending out vibrations in every moment. Your brain is a transmitter of your energy signature, and it is constantly emitting a signal into the field of life.

Living in freedom is embracing all of life. When you do, all the suffering, challenges, struggles, failures, deceptions, and lower vibratory worlds completely vanish. You sit on top of your mountain, viewing life for the first time from a new vantage point. You understand that everything you went through during the climb to higher consciousness was there to show you the path home to yourself. Every experience was necessary and perfectly orchestrated.

You've spent years preparing yourself for this world of freedom. As you settle into the new life you've designed, you know to say, "Yes" when life presents you with an opportunity.

The development and nurturing of your mind and soul is your responsibility. Ultimately, your destiny is in your hands. Living in the Freedom Frequency is your Divine power to transform all relationships and your life.

The world of fear will still exist around you. Those you encounter and the many forms of mass media will constantly remind you of other realities. Discover your own truths. Keep your focus on creating heaven on earth for you, your family, your community, and the world.

I trust that after reading these pages, you're *fired up* about life! I feel this book represents a piece of my own life's puzzle. I have held back in publishing this book for many years. Now I say, "YES" as I shine my light out into the world to connect with you.

I honour you as you shine your light and make your choice to live in the Freedom Frequency of life. Enjoy the journey home, the journey home to your heart. You are here to spiral up and fly high.

Together We Rise!

Karen of the Klassen family

Recommended Resources

- The mission of the Institute of HeartMath is to help establish heart-based living and global coherence by inspiring us all to connect with the intelligence and guidance of our own hearts. Receive free tools and resources by visiting www.heartmath.org

- *New York Times* best-selling author Gregg Braden is internationally renowned as a pioneer in bridging science, spirituality, and the real world. www.greggbraden.com

- Thoughts and words carry a vibration that can either destroy or create harmony. Thanks to the experimental work of Dr. Masaru Emoto, we can look to water, and its crystals, to confirm the transformative power of beautiful music, positive thinking, uplifting speech, and prayer. http://www.masaru-emoto.net/english

- David Wolfe is a Health, Nutrition, and Superfood Expert. Information on high vibrational foods and the benefits of eating raw food are available at: http://www.longevitywarehouse.com

- Together We Rise Course available at www.karenklassen.ca

Silent No More

In meditation I fly
Stumbling upon the truths that are I
The light is so bright inside
I cannot hide
I accept my lessons
Learn to apply
Experiences of unpleasantness I face
Becoming one with dignity and grace
Mother Gaia I have known
In every life I have been born
To seek the wisdom from within
I have the answers
I create
To become one with Source is never too late
Love is the key
To the door once closed in me
In the cycle of life
In the journey of remembering
To find I AM Divine perfection
I can no longer remain silent
For my brothers and sisters
Arise from your sleep
It is now time to go within, go deep, go deep
The heart, the soul does call
There we find our connectedness to all

By Karen of the Klassen family

About the Author

Karen of the Klassen family is an Inspirational Speaker, Leadership Facilitator and a Breakthrough Coach who reminds you that there is a higher love and wisdom within you that can dissolve all mental, emotional, and physical pain so you can integrate with the highest version of who you are.

The Together We Rise Journey is a powerful course offered each year as Karen empowers you to live above the line. You can register at karenklassen.ca

Karen's mission has evolved. She is co-founder of Life Force Canada, a movement of many conscious and aware sovereigns who have come together to create a parallel system that is for us all and by us all.

Manufactured by Amazon.ca
Bolton, ON